VISUAL QUICKSTART GUIDE

GARAGEBAND

FOR MAC OS X

Victor Gavenda

Peachpit Press

Visual QuickStart Guide
GarageBand For Mac OS X
Victor Gavenda

Peachpit Press

1249 Eighth Street
Berkeley, CA 94710
510/524-2178
800/283-9444
510/524-2221 (fax)

Find us on the World Wide Web at: www.peachpit.com
To report errors, please send a note to errata@peachpit.com

Peachpit Press is a division of Pearson Education

Editor: Judy Ziajka
Project Editor: Becky Morgan
Production Editor: Becky Winter
Copyeditor: Judy Ziajka
Technical Editor: Jeff Tolbert
Composition: Debbie Roberti, Myrna Vladic, Rick Gordon
Index: FireCrystal Communications
Cover Design: The Visual Group
Cover Production: George Mattingly / GMD

Notice of Rights

Notice of Liability

Trademarks

ISBN 0-321-27281-1

9 8 7 6 5 4 3 2 1

Printed and bound in the United States of America

Dedication

To my muses, Linda and Emma

Acknowledgments

Special thanks to:

Nancy Aldrich-Ruenzel, Peachpit Press's intrepid publisher, for giving me the chance to do this book. Now, if only I could get her to come to choir rehearsal more often…

Nancy Davis, Cliff Colby, and Marjorie Baer, acquisitions editors at Peachpit, for supporting my proposal for this book. Baked goods for everyone!

Becky Morgan, my Peachpit editor, for guiding me gently through the Way of the VQS. I am also grateful for her comfortable words during the stressful times.

Judy Ziajka, my development editor, for patiently fixing my bad writing habits over and over. Amazingly, she always understood better than I what I meant to say.

Jeff Tolbert, my technical editor, for many helpful suggestions and corrections. He saved me from embarrassing myself in print on several occasions.

Becky Winter, my production editor, and her crack team of compositors: Debbie Roberti, Myrna Vladic, and Rick Gordon. Their skill and hard work are responsible for making this book a pleasure to look at.

My colleague, Rebecca Gulick, for the loan of a valuable antique electric guitar (well, that's what I told the guy at the pawn shop…).

Rebecca's husband, Steve Dampier, for the fine line drawings in Chapter 5.

Reinel Adajar of Digidesign, for graciously agreeing to supply the photo of the Mbox used in Chapter 5.

TABLE OF CONTENTS

TABLE OF CONTENTS

Part 1:
Getting Music into GarageBand

GARAGEBAND OVERVIEW

Though it had long been rumored that Apple had a music creation iApp in the works, the announcement of GarageBand at Macworld 2004 sent waves of delight through the Mac music community.

Every Macintosh computer, starting with that adorable little 128K model in 1984, has shipped with some kind of audio hardware built in (unlike many Wintel machines), and Mac users have been in the forefront of the computer music revolution. Yet not all has been smooth sailing. Getting external audio or MIDI hardware to work with your Mac has often been a titanic struggle between man (or woman) and machine, and recording and sequencing software can be so complex that the documentation resembles the pilot's manual for the space shuttle. For many ordinary folks, performing and recording music on their Macs has always seemed just out of reach.

But GarageBand (with a little help from Mac OS X)—with its streamlined interface (one window, and one window *only*) and seamless integration with your Mac's audio hardware—is finally: music software for the rest of us.

What GarageBand Does

There is nothing radically new or revolutionary in anything that GarageBand does. Instead, in typical Apple fashion, it combines the most commonly used functions from a host of music applications into one program. Then it sweetens the deal by packaging the whole thing in a straightforward, unintimidating interface.

GarageBand provides one-stop shopping for all of your musical needs. In this one program you can:

- Compose songs using loops.

- Record live performers through a microphone or by plugging an electric guitar or bass into your Mac (what GarageBand calls *Real Instruments*).

- Record performances on MIDI instruments attached to the computer (called *Software Instruments* in GarageBand lingo).

- Edit MIDI data.

- Write songs that make use of all of the above.

GarageBand also provides extensive mixing and arranging tools. And when your magnum opus is complete, you can export it to your iTunes playlist so it's available for sharing with your friends or with the world.

But as the late-night infomercials say, "That's not all!"

Apple ships GarageBand with a treasure trove of musical goodies to help get you started:

- Over 1,000 Apple Loops.

- More than 50 high-quality Software Instruments, which use both synthesized sounds and sounds sampled from real-world instruments.

◆ Dozens of effects that you can apply to your recorded tracks, including 200 professional-level presets.

And if all that isn't enough, for an extra $99 you can buy Apple's GarageBand Jam Pack, a DVD crammed with 2,000 more Apple Loops, over 100 new Software Instruments, another 100 audio effects presets, and 15 guitar amp settings.

Enough talk. Let's take a look at this very cool sandbox Apple has made for us to play in.

Easy Does It

Throughout this book, I assume that you allowed the iLife '04 Installer program to perform an Easy Install operation. This option installs all of the iLife '04 programs in the Applications folder on your system disk. It also performs a few housekeeping chores, such as these:

◆ Adds an icon to the Dock for each iLife application.

◆ Places certain important files in the Library folder at the root level of your hard disk. This is where, for example, GarageBand expects to find its Apple Loops and Software Instruments. Don't move them!

◆ Creates a folder called GarageBand in the Music folder within your Home folder. This is the default location for saving songs you create in GarageBand. In official Mac OS X jargon, the path to this folder is ~/Music/GarageBand, where the tilde (~) represents your Home folder, or /Users/ [*your username*]/.

Launching GarageBand

Apple provides several ways to start GarageBand. As it launches, the program opens the song you were working on the last time it was running. The first time you start GarageBand, the process is a little different: GarageBand gives you several choices to get underway.

To launch GarageBand:

◆ *Do one of the following:*

▲ Open the Applications folder on your hard drive and double-click the GarageBand icon (**Figure 1.1**).

▲ Click the GarageBand icon in the Dock (**Figure 1.2**).

If you have opened GarageBand before, the main GarageBand window appears, showing the last song you worked on.

If this is your first time launching GarageBand, the Welcome to GarageBand dialog opens, giving you three choices (**Figure 1.3**):

▲ Open Existing Song presents you with a standard Open dialog. Use it to navigate to the song file you wish to open.

▲ Quit exits the program. Use it if you decide that now's not the time for a GarageBand session.

▲ Create New Song starts a brand-new song file. We'll talk about creating new songs in Chapter 2.

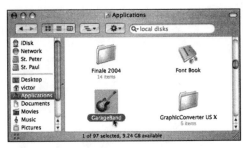

Figure 1.1 GarageBand, at home in the Applications folder.

Figure 1.2 GarageBand at large, hanging out in the Dock.

Figure 1.3 This friendly dialog greets you the first time you start GarageBand.

Figure 1.4 The main page of the online Help file.

Getting Help

GarageBand, alas, does not come with a printed manual. But, then, you already knew that, didn't you? That's why you're here, after all.

Apple does ship some fine online help with the program, as well as some tutorials to get you started on your first songs. The Help file even includes links to Apple's support Web site for answers to your more perplexing questions.

To use the online Help system:

1. Choose Help > GarageBand Help (Command-?).

   The Help Viewer application opens and displays the GarageBand Help file (**Figure 1.4**).

2. *Do one of the following:*

   ▲ Click the Contents link to view the list of topics covered in the file.

   ▲ Follow the Learn About GarageBand link to find tutorials and other documents in PDF format.

   ▲ Click the Solving Problems link to troubleshoot problems.

   ▲ Click the link under the "GarageBand Help" title to go to the main GarageBand Web page at Apple's Web site.

GETTING HELP

The GarageBand Interface

When you start GarageBand, a single large window gobbles up most of your screen (**Figure 1.5**). The window displays the contents of a single song; you can have only one song open at a time. Designwise, it owes much to its older sibling Soundtrack, from which much of GarageBand's code is derived. The faux-walnut strips along each side are unique to GarageBand, however. Apparently, the designers meant to recall the look of 1960s audio hardware. Groovy!

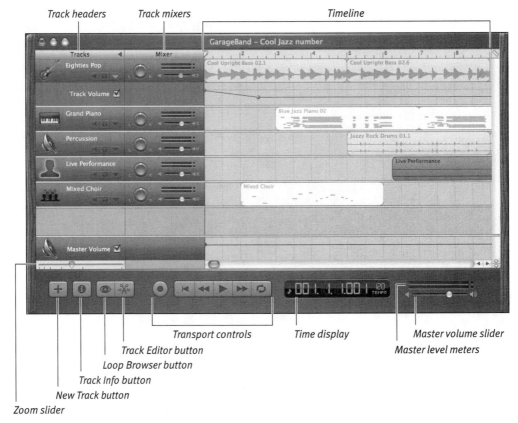

Figure 1.5 The GarageBand window in all its glory.

Figure 1.6 The loop browser, in button view.

Figure 1.7 The track editor, showing a Real Instrument track.

Most of the window is laid out as a grid. Each horizontal row represents a single track in your song. The leftmost column contains the *track headers*, which identify each track by name and instrument icon. In the second column you'll find the *track mixer* for each track. These contain controls for the track's volume and pan position (where the track seems to sit in the stereo field), as well as level meters that show changes in the track's volume as the track is played.

The lion's share of the window is taken up with the *timeline*, which displays the actual data that makes up your song. It's complex enough that it rates its own section, right after this one.

At the bottom of the Tracks column, you'll find the *zoom slider*. Use this to display more or less detail in the timeline. (I'll describe how the zoom slider works later in this chapter.)

Various controls for working with the tracks in the timeline live along its bottom edge. (You'll learn how to use them in Chapter 3.) The button with the plus sign (+) is the *Add Track button*; click it to add a new track to the timeline. The button with the circled *i* opens the *Track Info window*, which you use to set parameters for each track.

Clicking either the Loop Browser or Track Editor button causes a new pane to grow up out of the lower edge of the GarageBand window. (Click either button again to close the pane.) The button bearing the eye icon opens the *loop browser*, which you use to search for loops for your song (**Figure 1.6**). I'll describe it in more detail in Chapter 4. Click its neighbor, the button with the scissors icon, to open the *track editor* (**Figure 1.7**). The track editor takes different forms, depending on whether a Real Instrument track or a Software Instrument track is

continues on next page

selected. Skip to Chapter 9 to read more about the track editor.

Next comes a group of buttons that look just like controls you might see on a VCR or a CD player (**Figure 1.8**). These are the *transport controls*, and they allow you to move through the timeline and hear different parts of your song. The round *Record button* starts and stops recording. The next four buttons are self-explanatory: *Go to Beginning*, *Rewind*, *Play*, and *Fast Forward*. The last of the transport controls, the *Cycle button*, turns the cycle region on and off (see Chapters 6 and 7 to learn about the cycle region). The buttons turn a vivid blue when engaged (except for the Record button, which turns traffic-light red).

The numerical readout is the *time display*. It shows you where the playhead is in the timeline. You can choose whether time is displayed in absolute time (hours, minutes, seconds, and fractions) or as musical time (measures, beats, and ticks). The tempo of the song is also shown here. (If you need help with any of these musical terms, read the sections "About Tempo" and "About Time Signatures" in Chapter 2.) To learn more, see "Using the Time Display" later in this chapter.

At the lower right of the window, the horizontal line with the pearlescent slider is the *master volume slider*. The pair of colored bars above it are the *master level meters* for the song as a whole. While you mix and arrange your song, be sure to watch these meters and make sure they don't bump into the right end of the meter too often (recording engineers call it "going into the red"). If they do, you'll hear distortion, or *clipping*. This is not the good kind of distortion, like on a Rolling Stones record, but really horrendous-sounding digital distortion. For more about setting the song's final volume level, see Chapter 11.

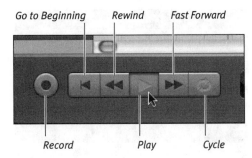

Go to Beginning   Rewind   Fast Forward

Record   Play   Cycle

Figure 1.8 The transport controls work just like the buttons on your VCR.

Figure 1.9 Drag this corner of the window to resize the window.

Figure 1.10 Clicking the zoom button snaps the GarageBand window to the edges of your screen.

✔ Tip

- While playing a song, don't use the master volume slider to adjust the volume purely for your listening pleasure. Use your computer's volume control instead.

To resize the GarageBand window:

◆ Drag the lower-right corner of the window up and to the left to shrink the window (**Figure 1.9**); drag down and to the right to enlarge it.

✔ Tip

- To enlarge the GarageBand window to fill your entire display in one quick stroke, click the green zoom button in the window's upper-left corner (**Figure 1.10**). To snap the window back to its former size, click the button again.

Anatomy of the Timeline

The timeline is where the magic happens (**Figure 1.11**). Here's where you record Real and Software Instruments into individual tracks, add loops, and arrange regions. Right now, I'll just identify the pieces; in the next section, I'll show you how to operate the controls.

Running along the top of the timeline is the *beat ruler*, calibrated in measures and beats. The *playhead* (a vertical bar with a triangular top) moves along the ruler as the song is played, showing the point in the song being heard at any given moment. The playhead also indicates where cut and copied items will be pasted in the timeline. The *Timeline Grid button* lives at the right end of the ruler. Clicking this button displays a pop-up menu from which you can choose the units displayed on the ruler. (You'll learn more about the timeline grid later in this chapter).

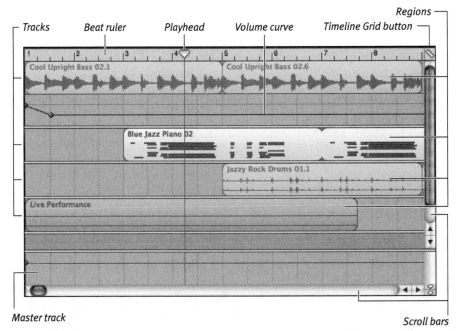

Figure 1.11 The timeline, where the pieces of your song come together.

Most of the timeline is taken up with *tracks*, which represent different layers of musical data in your song. When you add loops to your song, they're placed in tracks. Likewise, when you record Real or Software Instruments, the recordings appear here, in tracks. Finally, you fine-tune, or arrange, your song by adjusting loops and regions of tracks here. We'll dig more deeply into the mysteries of tracks in Chapter 3.

Tracks may be empty, or they may contain colored, rounded rectangles, called *regions*. Each region represents a recorded passage (either Real or Software Instrument) or a loop that has been dragged to the timeline. To give your song its final shape, you'll work with these regions. You can cut, copy, or paste regions; you can move or resize them; and you can transpose them. Regions are discussed in detail in Chapter 8.

Each track has a *volume curve*. By adding and adjusting control points along the curve, you can shape the dynamics of the track. Similarly, the song as a whole has a *master track*, which governs the dynamic level of the total of all the tracks. You can also use the master track to add special effects to your song. You'll learn more about volume curves and the master track in Chapter 11.

To move around in the timeline, drag the *scroll bars* at the bottom and right edges of the timeline. Dragging the bottom scroll bar moves you in time; the vertical scroll bar appears only if the song contains so many tracks that they can't all be displayed at once. Drag up and down on the vertical scroll bar to see the rest of your tracks.

ANATOMY OF THE TIMELINE

Working in the Timeline

The timeline is the part of the interface that holds all the parts of your song and keeps them in the proper order. Usually, your entire song won't fit onto the screen all at once; that's why GarageBand thoughtfully supplies many techniques for moving around in your song and for adjusting the amount of your song that you can see at once.

To work efficiently in GarageBand, you need to become proficient in using the timeline to zip from one part of your song to another. Doing this involves moving the playhead, which you can do in several ways. As you'll see, you can move the playhead directly, on the beat ruler, or you can use the transport controls. You can also use the time display. For the nimble-fingered, there are also keyboard shortcuts (**Table 1.1**).

To move the playhead directly using the beat ruler:

◆ *Do one of the following:*

▲ Drag the triangle at the top of the playhead to the desired spot on the beat ruler (**Figure 1.12**).

▲ Click a spot on the beat ruler to move the playhead to that position.

Figure 1.12 Drag the playhead to move it along the timeline.

Table 1.1

Keyboard Shortcuts for Moving the Playhead	
ACTION	KEY COMBINATION
Start/pause playback	Spacebar
Go to start of song	Home or Z
Go to end of song	End or Option-Z
Move backward one measure	Left arrow
Move forward one measure	Right arrow
Move backward a full screen	Page Up
Move forward a full screen	Page Down

WORKING IN THE TIMELINE

To move the playhead using the transport controls:

◆ Review Figure 1.8; *do one of the following:*

▲ Click the Play button to start song playback. Click the button again to pause playback.

▲ Click the Go to Beginning button to jump the playhead to the start of the song.

▲ Click the Rewind or Fast Forward button to move the playhead backward or forward through the song one measure at a time.

▲ Hold down the mouse on the Rewind or Fast Forward button to move quickly backward or forward through the song.

WORKING IN THE TIMELINE

Using the Time Display

The time display provides a constant read-out of the position of the playhead. You can also use it to move the playhead to a precise moment in time. By default, time is displayed in musical units, but you can switch to an absolute time display if you wish.

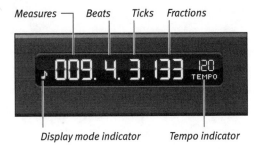

Figure 1.13 The time display, in musical time format.

▲ **Musical time (Figure 1.13):**
Normally, the time display readout tells you where the playhead is in relation to the metric structure of the song. The numbers indicate the measure, beat, tick, and fractions of a beat. The tiny eighth note in the lower-left corner of the display indicates that musical units are in use.

A *tick* is equivalent to a sixteenth note. Most songs use the quarter note as the beat, in which case there are 4 ticks to a beat. The three-digit number in the fractions field is a little more obscure. There are 240 of these fractions in a tick. Because 4 × 240 = 960, a fraction represents about one one-thousandth of a beat. Don't worry—it's not often that you'll need to locate the playhead with such precision!

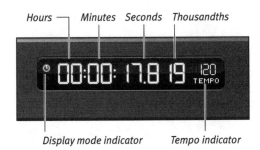

Figure 1.14 The time display, set to show absolute time.

▲ **Absolute time (Figure 1.14):** If the music you're composing is intended to be a part of a nonmusical project—if, for example, you're scoring a film—you'll find the absolute time display very handy. It greatly simplifies the process of fitting a piece of music to the length of a movie scene. Time is displayed in this format:

hours : minutes : seconds . thousandths of seconds.

You can tell that the display is recording absolute time because a miniature clock appears in its upper-left corner.

Figure 1.15 Top: Position the mouse pointer over the almost-invisible eighth note. Bottom: After you click, the time display is in absolute time format.

The time display also shows the tempo of the song. *Tempo* refers to the speed or pace of the song. It's measured in *beats per minute*, or *bpm*. The tempo readout doubles as a control for adjusting the song's tempo. For more about tempo, see Chapter 2.

To change the format of the time display:

◆ *Do one of the following:*

▲ If the display shows absolute time, click the eighth note, barely visible below the clock, to switch to musical time (**Figure 1.15**).

▲ If the display shows musical time, click the faint clock icon, just above the eighth note, to change to absolute time.

To move the playhead using the time display:

◆ *Do one of the following:*

▲ Drag up or down on any of the numbers in the time display to increase or decrease the value of the number.

▲ Double-click the number you want to change to select it. It will blink to show that it is selected. Type a new number and press Return.

USING THE TIME DISPLAY

To adjust the tempo:

1. Place the mouse pointer over the tempo indicator and press the mouse button.

   The tempo slider appears (**Figure 1.16**).

2. Drag down to lower the tempo and slow down the song (**Figure 1.17**), or drag upward to speed up the tempo. The available values range from 60 to 240 bpm.

✔ Tip

- If you're using a PowerBook, you'll notice that the Home, Page Up, Page Down, and End commands are on the arrow keys. To get these commands to work, you have to hold down the Fn key (at the lower left of the keyboard) while pressing an arrow key.

  For example, to access the Home function, press Fn-left arrow.

Figure 1.16 Whoa—176 bpm is way too fast for the rock ballad we're writing. Let's dial things back a notch or two.

Figure 1.17 Ah! That's more like it. A nice, mellow 84 bpm suits the piece much better.

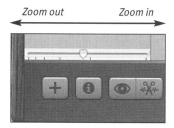

Zoom out   Zoom in

Figure 1.18 The zoom slider.

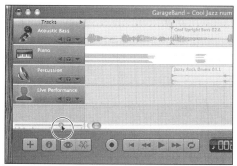

Figure 1.19 Top: The timeline set to a moderate level of zoom. Bottom: With the zoom slider dragged far to the right, much more detail is visible in the tracks.

Zooming in the Timeline

From time to time, you'll want to change the level of detail at which you view your song. Sometimes, a broad overview is just what you need; sometimes, you need to get in close. The zoom slider (**Figure 1.18**) is just the tool for the job.

To zoom into the timeline:

◆ Drag the zoom slider to the right (or press Control-right arrow) to magnify your view of the timeline (**Figure 1.19**).

To zoom out from the timeline:

◆ Drag the zoom slider left (or press Control-left arrow) to zoom out for a bird's-eye view of your song.

✔ Tip

■ Instead of dragging the slider, you can jump to a zoom level by clicking a spot on the scale.

About the Timeline Grid

As you build your song, you'll stack loops and recorded music on top of each other, to create a rich texture. Normally, you'll want to make sure that events in different tracks are aligned in time. GarageBand provides a timeline grid to help you maintain this alignment. There's a timeline grid in the track editor, but we'll save that subject for Chapter 9.

When the timeline grid is turned on, these operations snap to the nearest grid location in the timeline:

◆ Moving the playhead.

◆ Moving the cycle region.

◆ Placing loops into the timeline.

◆ Moving regions.

◆ Resizing regions.

◆ Moving the control points on volume and controller curves in the track editor.

The grid is visible in the tracks and the beat ruler. In the beat ruler, the grid takes the form of faint gray tick marks between the beat markers. Gridlines extend across the full width of tracks devoid of music data. If you choose an extremely small grid value, however, only the beat ruler will show all of the divisions. Only the larger divisions will be displayed in the tracks, to avoid cluttering the interface (**Figure 1.20**). The grid display also depends on the current zoom level. At higher zoom levels, more of the grid's detail is displayed.

You'll usually want to keep the grid in force, but if you crave more creative freedom, you can turn it off. The command is a simple toggle; to turn the grid back on, just repeat the action.

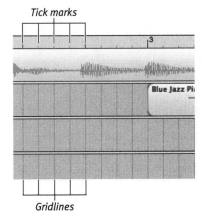

Tick marks

Gridlines

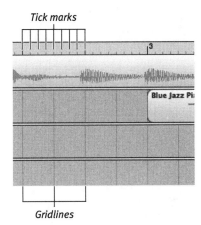

Tick marks

Gridlines

Figure 1.20 Top: The grid setting is $\frac{1}{16}$ notes. Both the beat ruler and track gridlines show four divisions per beat. Bottom: The grid setting is $\frac{1}{32}$ notes. Now the beat ruler shows eight divisions per beat, but the gridline display has been streamlined to show only two divisions per beat.

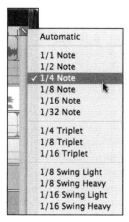

Figure 1.21 The timeline grid menu.

To disable or enable the timeline grid:

◆ *Do one of the following:*

▲ Choose Control > Snap to Grid to uncheck (or recheck) the command and turn the grid off (or on).

▲ Press Command-G.

Choosing a value for the timeline grid

You can set the grid to any of these note values:

◆ $^1/_1$ notes (whole notes), $^1/_2$ notes, $^1/_4$ notes, $^1/_8$ notes, $^1/_{16}$ notes, $^1/_{32}$ notes.

◆ $^1/_4$ note triplets, $^1/_8$ note triplets, $^1/_{16}$ note triplets.

◆ $^1/_8$ note swing light, $^1/_8$ note swing heavy, $^1/_{16}$ note swing light, $^1/_{16}$ note swing heavy.

The smaller the note value, the finer the grid. The triplet settings push the subdivisions of the beat away from an even split toward an uneven split, with a ratio of 3:2. This lends a gentle swing to the rhythm. The swing settings do the same thing, but more noticeably, with the heavy settings having the strongest effect.

By default, GarageBand uses the Automatic setting, which resizes the grid according to the current zoom level. As you zoom into or out from the timeline, the grid setting adjusts to smaller and larger values, respectively.

To choose a value for the timeline grid:

1. Click the Timeline Grid button at the upper right of the timeline.

   The timeline grid menu appears (**Figure 1.21**).

2. Choose one of the settings from the menu.

WORKING WITH SONGS

The *song* is the unit of creation in GarageBand. Whether you've expended hours of blood, sweat, and tears giving voice to your singular inspiration, or whether you're just noodling around with no specific goal in mind, a song is your finished product. Whenever GarageBand is running, there is one song open: no more, no less. If you close the song without opening another, the application quits. This helps to keep things simple.

This chapter covers the basics of dealing with songs, including:

◆ Opening, saving, and playing songs.

◆ Starting a new song from scratch and choosing its tempo, time signature, and key.

◆ Setting a song's length.

◆ Undoing your work when you realize you've made a mistake.

About Songs

You build your song in the timeline, creating *tracks* in the timeline to contain the various chunks of audio data that go into your song. You add Apple Loops (that use either Real or Software Instruments) to your song by dragging them to tracks. You record Real Instruments and Software Instruments into tracks. See Chapter 3 for more about tracks.

Each item that you've added to your song, whether it's a loop or 30 seconds of recorded sound, is called a *region* in GarageBand-speak. You refine the overall shape of your creation by *arranging* these regions (which I'll discuss in Chapter 8). Regions can be lengthened or shortened; looped, split, or joined; and moved around within a track or moved from one track to another.

The track editor, a more advanced feature of GarageBand, allows you to edit the fundamental characteristics of regions (more about this in Chapter 9). Using the track editor, you can change a region's name or transpose a region to another key (except for Real Instrument regions that consist of audio you record yourself). You can even edit the individual notes of Software Instrument regions.

Finally, you refine your song's *mix*, setting each track's volume and stereo position, and adding effects (discussed in Chapter 10) and adjusting the overall volume level of the song (mixing is covered in Chapter 11). Then you're ready to share your magnum opus with the world. Use the Export to iTunes command (explained in Chapter 12) to consolidate all of your tracks into a single audio file, which is output to your iTunes library. From there, you can burn your song to a CD, post it to a Web site, or copy it to your iPod.

Figure 2.1 This dialog gives you one last chance to save changes to your song before you open another.

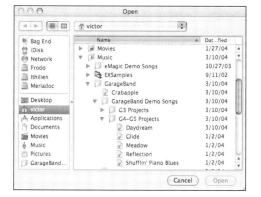

Figure 2.2 The ever-popular Open dialog.

Figure 2.3 A song open in GarageBand.

Opening a Song

Opening a song file in GarageBand is pretty standard procedure, but closing a file may throw you for a loop (so to speak). If you use the File > Close command (Command-W), the song will close, but so will the program. GarageBand is not at all happy unless a song file is open.

If you want to quit working on one song and switch to another, don't use the Close command. Instead, use the Open command to open a different song file.

To open a song:

1. Choose File > Open (Command-O).

   If you have made changes to the song that is currently open since the last time you saved it, you'll get a warning (**Figure 2.1**). Click Don't Save to discard the changes, or Cancel to abort the Open command and continue working in the same song, or Save to save the changes you've made.

   The Open dialog appears (**Figure 2.2**).

2. Navigate to the folder containing your GarageBand songs. By default, this is ~/Music/GarageBand.

3. Select the desired song and click Open.

   The song and its tracks appear in the GarageBand window (**Figure 2.3**).

continues on next page

OPENING A SONG

✔ Tips

- GarageBand automatically keeps track of the last few songs you've opened. To re-open a song you were just working on, choose File > Open Recent and select a song from the submenu (**Figure 2.4**). If you're tired of seeing the same old song titles, choose Clear Menu from the same submenu to wipe the slate clean and start afresh.

- Be careful! If you start to open a song but change your mind and click the Cancel button, you'll get a scolding message from the program (**Figure 2.5**). See? I told you GarageBand gets cranky if it doesn't have a song to display. Open or create a song, or just click Quit and call it a day.

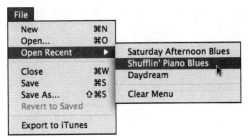

Figure 2.4 Use the Open Recent command to re-open a song you worked on before.

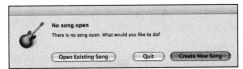

Figure 2.5 GarageBand doesn't like it when you don't have a song open.

Disclosure button

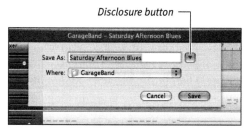

Figure 2.6 The minimal Save As dialog.

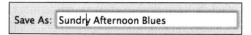

Figure 2.7 Rename your song by typing here.

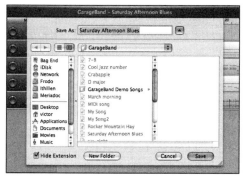

Figure 2.8 After you click the disclosure button, the Save As dialog expands to reveal more features.

Saving a Song

If you have any experience with computers, you don't need reminding of this simple truth: Your computer, yes, even your lovely Macintosh, will crash when it is most inconvenient. Or GarageBand will suddenly vanish from the screen and leave you with nothing but one of those maddening "Unexpectedly Quit" messages.

So please remember to save your work often.

To save a song to disk:

◆ Choose File > Save (Command-S).

To save your song with a different name:

1. Choose File > Save As (Command-Shift-S).
   The Save As dialog (in its minimal form) drops down from the GarageBand window's title bar (**Figure 2.6**).

2. Type a new name for the song in the Save As field (**Figure 2.7**).

3. The program always assumes that you want to save the song in the default GarageBand folder in your Music folder. If you want to save a song elsewhere, choose one of the locations in the Where pop-up menu (Figure 2.6).

4. Click Save or press Return.

✔ Tip

■ The list of folders in the Where pop-up menu is pretty limited. If you want to be able to navigate to any folder on your hard disk, click the disclosure button to the right of the Save As field. The expanded version of the Save As dialog appears (**Figure 2.8**). This allows you to navigate to any folder on your computer. Click the disclosure button again to shrink the dialog back to its minimal form.

SAVING A SONG

27

About Filename Extensions

One feature that distinguishes Mac OS X from earlier Mac operating systems is its greater reliance on filename suffixes, or *extensions*, to associate documents with the applications that created them. GarageBand, for example, will open only files whose filenames end in the extension *.band.*

Fortunately, you don't have to worry about this detail. GarageBand automatically appends the extension to every song you create or save. Furthermore, both GarageBand and Mac OS X are designed to protect you from inadvertently damaging your files by keeping their extensions hidden.

GarageBand does offer a peek behind the curtain. You can uncheck the Hide Extensions box in the Save As dialog (**Figure 2.9**), but that shows you the extension only on the filename currently occupying the Save As field.

If you're curious about extensions, you can configure the Finder so it displays all of your files with their extensions exposed to the elements. In the Finder, choose Finder > Preferences (Command-,) and click the Advanced button. Then check the Show All File Extensions box (**Figure 2.10**).

But remember: look—don't touch!

Figure 2.9 Uncheck the Hide Extensions box to reveal the *.band* extension on your song's name.

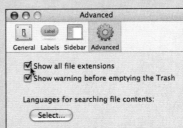

Figure 2.10 Use the Advanced pane of the Finder Preferences dialog to turn on the display of all filename extensions.

Figure 2.11 Click this button to play the song.

Playing a Song

What's the use of having a fancy music program if you can't listen to the tunes you create? Don't worry—it's easy to play a song in GarageBand.

To play a song:

◆ Make sure the song you want to hear is open. *Then do one of the following:*

▲ Click the Play button under the time-line (**Figure 2.11**).

▲ Press the spacebar.

To pause playback, click the Play button or press the spacebar again.

Use the other transport controls (described in Chapter 1) to navigate through your song.

Creating a New Song

When you start a new song in GarageBand, you're asked to set some basic parameters that will apply to the song as a whole. As you'll learn in Chapter 3, in the section "Working with the Master Track," it's possible to change these settings later, after you've worked on the song for a while. Doing this can have unpredictable results, however, so it's best to set up the song the way you want it from the beginning.

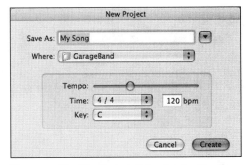

Figure 2.12 The New Project dialog (minimal form).

To create a new song:

1. Choose File > New (Command-N).

    If you've made changes to the song you're working on but haven't saved the document recently, you'll be asked if you want to save first (Figure 2.1). Click Save.

    The New Project dialog appears (**Figure 2.12**).

2. Type a name for your song in the Save As field.

3. Choose a location for the song *by doing one of the following:*

    ▲ Make a selection from the Where pop-up menu.

    ▲ Click the disclosure button to display the expanded form of the New Project dialog (**Figure 2.13**). Now you're free to save your song anywhere you like.

4. Choose a tempo, time signature, and key for your song, according to the criteria described in the next sections.

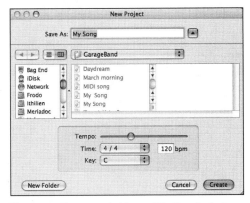

Figure 2.13 The expanded form of the New Project dialog.

5. Click Create.

The New Project dialog closes, and a new GarageBand window opens, showing a song containing a single empty Grand Piano Software Instrument track (**Figure 2.14**).

✔ Tip

■ The vast majority of GarageBand songs that have been posted to Web sites since the appearance of the program use the default tempo, time signature, and key settings for a new song. The simplest thing you can do to demonstrate your creativity and individuality is to promise yourself *never* to use this combination of settings. Future generations will thank you.

Figure 2.14 A freshly minted song file: a blank slate ready to record your musical thoughts.

About Tempo

Chapter 1 touched briefly on the subject of tempo. The word *tempo*, like many bits of musical jargon, comes from Italian. Translated literally, it means *time*. In music, it refers to the speed, or pace, of a piece of music. Tempo can be described in terms of how a piece feels: blues ballads have a slow tempo; punk rock songs have a fast, driving tempo. But tempo can also be described in numerical terms. Tempo is measured in beats per minute (bpm), where a *beat* is the background rhythmic pulse of a song. In GarageBand, you can choose any tempo between 60 and 240 bpm.

Your choice of tempo has a profound effect on the emotional content of your song. A fast tempo (also called an up-tempo beat) gets the blood pumping and is a feature of dance and rock 'n' roll music. Slower tempos set a mellower mood and are often found in hip-hop songs and ballads from any genre.

Each GarageBand song can have only one tempo, which remains in force through the entire song. The tempo you set affects mainly loops and Software Instrument recordings. It has no effect on Real Instrument recordings you add to your song.

To set the song's tempo:

◆ Working in the New Project dialog, *do one of the following:*

▲ Drag the Tempo slider left to choose a slower tempo; drag to the right to choose a faster one (**Figure 2.15**). (Watch the bpm field below the slider.)

▲ Type the desired tempo directly into the bpm field.

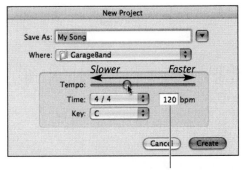

Current tempo

Figure 2.15 The Tempo slider and the current tempo readout, showing beats per minute.

About Time Signatures

In addition to setting the tempo to define the rhythmic character of your piece, you need to set the time signature. The tempo describes the speed at which the beats go by, but the time signature defines the grouping of those beats.

Beats are grouped together into *measures*. The beat is the rhythmic pulse of the song, and the measure organizes these beats into repeating patterns of accented (or strong) beats. Measures begin with a strong beat, which is called the *downbeat*. The time signature determines the number of beats in a measure and the kind of notes that represent those beats. Time signatures look like fractions in GarageBand: two numbers with a slash between them. The number on the left is the number of beats in a measure. The number on the right indicates what kind of note gets the beat.

For example, the most common time signature in pop music (and the default for a GarageBand song) is 4/4. This means that there are four beats in a measure, and that each beat is represented by a quarter note.

These are the time signatures available in GarageBand:

◆ 2/2

◆ 2/4, 3/4, 4/4, 5/4, 7/4

◆ 6/8, 7/8, 9/8, 12/8

Some of these are not very common in pop music. Three-quarter time—3/4—is used most famously for waltzes. Marches tend to be in 2/4 time. The time signature 6/8 is distinctive to folk music from the British Isles when used at a brisk tempo (think Irish jig);

continues on next page

ABOUT TIME SIGNATURES

taken at a slow tempo, you'll find 6/8 blues and jazz songs. The rest are rather obscure; you might encounter 7/8 or 7/4 time in some Eastern European folk music, and the others are used primarily by classical composers.

Just as with tempo, the time signature you choose remains in effect for the entire song. The time signature you set provides merely a metric framework for the song. There's nothing to stop you from adding to your song a Real Instrument or Software Instrument performance that uses a different time signature, although your song will remain in the original time signature.

To set the time signature:

◆ Working in the New Project dialog, choose the desired time signature from the Time pop-up menu (**Figure 2.16**).

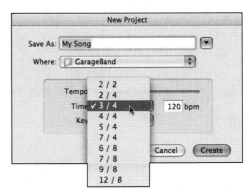

Figure 2.16 Choosing a time signature from the Time pop-up menu.

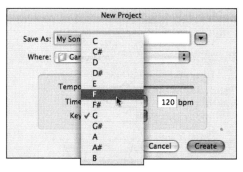

Figure 2.17 Choosing the key of F from the Key pop-up menu.

About Keys

Tempo and time signature together define the rhythmic structure of your song. Now we need to talk about another characteristic of music: pitch. For each song, you need to choose a *key*. A key consists of a main note (called the *tonic*) and a scale that begins on that note. A song in a particular key will, in general, begin on the tonic and end on that note. The chords that accompany the song will be made up mostly of notes in the scale that starts on the tonic.

For example, if you choose the key of C, most of the notes in the song will come from the scale: C D E F G A B C—the white keys on the piano.

The choice of key depends on many factors. Sometimes you choose a key to fit an individual singer's voice. For instrumental pieces, you might choose a key that's easy to play on that instrument (guitarists tend to like G and D, whereas pianists often feel comfortable in keys with lots of sharps, like D-flat or E).

GarageBand lets you pick a key based on any note, though for the black keys of the piano, it lists only the sharp version; for instance, if you want B-flat, choose A# (A-sharp) instead. Whichever key you choose remains in effect for the entire song. Like the time signature, the "official" key of the song has no effect on music you record; however, the Apple Loops that come with GarageBand are smart enough to adapt to the key you have chosen for your song.

To set the key:

◆ Working in the New Project dialog, choose the desired key from the Key pop-up menu (**Figure 2.17**).

About Song Length

When you create a new song, its length is automatically (and arbitrarily) set to 200 measures. If you record regions that extend beyond this limit, more measures are automatically added to accommodate the new material. When you export your song to iTunes, GarageBand includes only the measures up to the end of the final region in the song. In other words, if your last region ends at measure 176 but the song ends at 200, GarageBand trims the 24 empty measures from the end of the song. (More about this in Chapter 12.) You can also adjust the length of the song manually.

To change the length of a song:

1. Scroll to the end of your song and find the end-of-song marker. It's a purple triangle (**Figure 2.18**).

2. Drag the marker to the left to shorten the song (**Figure 2.19**), or drag to the right to lengthen it.

✔ Tip

■ When dragging the end-of-song marker, be very careful to place your mouse pointer exactly on the triangle. If you miss by even a little bit and click the beat ruler instead, the playhead will suddenly jump to that position. The playhead then covers up most of the end-of-song marker, making your task even harder (**Figure 2.20**).

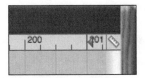

Figure 2.18 The end-of-song marker.

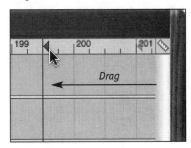

Figure 2.19 Dragging the marker left to trim some measures from the song.

Figure 2.20 Oops. Indiscriminate clicking can sometimes get you into trouble.

Figure 2.21 The Undo command.

Figure 2.22 Choosing the Revert to Saved command causes this warning to appear.

Undoing Your Work

Even the brightest and best among us make mistakes; that's why the Undo command exists. It lets you try out an adjustment to your song. If you don't like the result, you can return the song to its previous state. And because sometimes Undo is itself a mistake, you can use the Redo command to undo the Undo.

Then there are times when you suddenly realize that everything you've done to a song since you opened it has been a disaster, and you wish you could erase everything that's happened and go back to the saved version. That's what the Revert command is for.

To undo an action:

◆ Choose Edit > Undo [*name of the last action*] or press Command-Z (**Figure 2.21**).

To redo an action:

◆ Choose Edit > Redo [*name of the action that was undone*] or press Command-Shift-Z.

To go back to the last saved version of a song:

1. Choose File > Revert to Saved.

   An Alert dialog slides down from the GarageBand window's title bar (**Figure 2.22**).

2. Click Revert (or press Return) to undo all of the changes you have made to the song since you last saved it.

   If you decide to keep your changes intact after all, click Cancel (or press Command-. or Esc).

Multiple Undos

It's not mentioned in the documentation, but GarageBand supports multiple Undos. This means that, after using the Undo command, you can continue to issue further Undo commands and step backward through the history of your work in GarageBand.

Because the feature is undocumented, I don't know for sure how far you can retrace your steps. Another publisher's GarageBand book says that you can undo 10 steps, but on one occasion I was able to step back through 24 steps. But sometimes I can undo only 6 steps. Most likely, the number of possible undos is determined by the amount of RAM in your machine and the type of operations you are undoing. If you perform a series of steps that don't tax your machine's resources very much, then you can probably undo a good number of steps. If, on the other hand, you have performed some RAM-intensive operations, you will probably be able to undo fewer steps.

UNDOING YOUR WORK

WORKING WITH TRACKS

3

Most songs combine voices and instruments to create a layered texture. A typical song might include:

- ◆ Percussion supplying a pervasive background beat.

- ◆ A bass instrument providing a solid foundation for the harmony.

- ◆ A body of other instruments that fill out the harmony and add color to the sound.

- ◆ A solo instrument or vocal line that carries the main melody.

In GarageBand, you use tracks to organize these layers of sound. Each track has certain settings that remain constant for the length of the song, and that keep the character of the track consistent.

About Tracks

GarageBand associates each track with an "instrument." In GarageBand, this word really means "a source of musical data." Every track is either a Real Instrument track or a Software Instrument track. You can't record a Real Instrument into a Software Instrument track and vice versa. When you add a track, you first have to decide whether it will be a Real Instrument track or a Software Instrument track. And once you've chosen, you can't switch a track to the other flavor. Here's how to choose:

◆ Choose a Real Instrument track if you plan to use the track for audio recording.

◆ Choose a Software Instrument track if you plan to record from a MIDI device, such as a keyboard.

◆ Both kinds of tracks will accept loops, but you can drag Real Instrument loops only to a Real Instrument track. You can drag Software Instrument loops to either kind of track, but Software Instrument loops dragged to Real Instrument tracks are converted to Real Instrument regions.

Color Coding

Tracks and regions are color-coded in GarageBand to remind you of their type.

◆ Green tracks and regions use Software Instruments, both recordings and loops.

◆ Blue tracks use Real Instruments and can contain:

   ▲ Blue regions (Real Instrument loops).

   ▲ Purple regions (Real Instrument regions that consist of audio recordings).

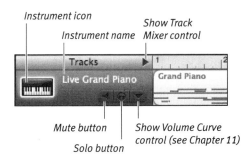

Instrument icon

Instrument name

Show Track Mixer control

Mute button

Solo button

Show Volume Curve control (see Chapter 11)

Figure 3.1 Track header

About the Track Header

Each track is identified by a track header, found in the Tracks column of the GarageBand window (**Figure 3.1**).

The header's principal features are the track's instrument name and icon.

The header also contains controls that govern the playback of individual tracks. The *Mute button* silences the track, and the *Solo button* allows the track to be heard alone.

Two of the controls in the track header reveal hidden interface elements that give access to more features of tracks. Clicking the triangle to the right of the word *Tracks* displays the track mixer (visible by default), which has controls for the volume level and pan position of individual tracks (see "About the Track Mixer" later in this chapter). The triangle to the right of the Solo button reveals the track's volume curve, which I'll describe in Chapter 11.

Selecting Tracks

Some operations involving tracks require that you first select the track in question. Selecting a track is a simple procedure. Only one track can be selected at a time.

To select a track:

◆ *Do one of the following:*

▲ Click the track header (**Figure 3.2**).

▲ Click any region within the track (**Figure 3.3**).

The header of the selected track acquires a color cast (green for Software Instruments, blue for Real Instruments), and the instrument icon starts to glow in the same color (**Figure 3.4**).

✔ Tip

■ When selecting a track, don't click within the empty, gray area of the track. That selects nothing.

To select an adjacent track using the keyboard:

◆ *Do one of the following:*

▲ Starting from a selected track, to select the next higher track, press the up arrow key.

▲ To select the next lower track, press the down arrow key.

Figure 3.2 Click the header of the track you wish to select.

Figure 3.3 Click a region in the desired track.

Figure 3.4 The header of a selected track.

Figure 3.5 The mouse pointer poised over the Mute button.

Figure 3.6 The Mute button is on.

Muting a Track

If you have one track that tends to over-power the rest, it can be helpful to silence it temporarily, while you work on the rest of the composition. Or if you want to refine the balance of your backup vocals, making the melody go away for a while can ease the process.

For these situations and others, the ability to mute a track comes in handy. You can mute more than one track at a time.

To mute a track:

◆ *Do one of the following:*

   ▲ Click the Mute button on the header of the track you wish to silence (**Figure 3.5**).

   ▲ Select the track you want to mute and press the M key.

   The Mute button lights up and the track is dimmed in the timeline, indicating that muting is in effect (**Figure 3.6**).

To unmute a muted track:

◆ *Do one of the following:*

   ▲ Click the track's Mute button.

   ▲ Select the muted track and press the M key.

   The Mute button darkens and the track is no longer dimmed, showing that the track is no longer muted.

MUTING A TRACK

Soloing a Track

You'll occasionally find it handy to isolate a single voice (or several voices) in your composition. This is called *soloing a track*. It's especially useful when recording a new track in a song whose texture is getting rather busy. You can set the drum track or the bass track to solo to provide a simple accompaniment while you record the new track.

You can set more than one track to solo at a time.

To solo a track:

◆ *Do one of the following:*

   ▲ Click the Solo button in the track's header (**Figure 3.7**).

   ▲ Select the track you want to hear as a solo and press the S key.

   The Solo button lights up and the other tracks are dimmed, indicating that muting is in effect (**Figure 3.8**).

To turn off soloing for a track:

◆ *Do one of the following:*

   ▲ Click the track's Solo button.

   ▲ Select the solo track and press the S key.

   The Solo button darkens and the other tracks are no longer dimmed, showing that the track is no longer set to solo.

Figure 3.7 Clicking the Solo button.

Figure 3.8 The Solo button is on.

Pan position control   *Level meters*

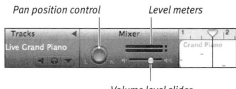

Volume level slider

Figure 3.9 The track mixer

Figure 3.10 Click this triangle to show the track mixer.

Figure 3.11 The track mixer slides out from behind the track header.

About the Track Mixer

Also associated with each track is another control panel, the track mixer (**Figure 3.9**). The track mixer may be hidden; if so, you'll need to reveal it so it can be used. Use the controls on the track mixer to set the pan position (where the track seems to come from in the stereo field) and volume for individual tracks. The volume level meters show the track's output volume. I'll discuss these controls in more detail when we talk about recording Real Instruments in Chapter 6 and mixing in Chapter 11.

To reveal the track mixer:

◆ If the track mixer is hidden, *do one of the following:*

 ▲ Click the right-pointing triangle at the top-right corner of the Tracks column (**Figure 3.10**).

 ▲ Press Command-Y.

 The track mixer slides out from behind the track header (**Figure 3.11**).

To hide the track mixer:

◆ If the track mixer is visible, *do one of the following:*

 ▲ Click the left-pointing triangle at the top-right corner of the Tracks column.

 ▲ Press Command-Y.

 The track mixer disappears.

Real vs. Software Instrument Tracks

The two types of tracks used in GarageBand correspond to the two methods of recording musical information:

◆ Real Instrument tracks use recorded audio.

◆ Software Instrument tracks use MIDI (Musical Instrument Digital Interface) data.

Each of these track types has its advantages and disadvantages, and each one comes from different source material.

Audio data consists of recordings of actual instruments or voices, captured with a microphone or a guitar pickup or similar electronic pickup. Such a recording stores a replica of the original sound in your GarageBand song, so when you play it back, you hear something that sounds just like the original. Because the original sound is reproduced with a high degree of precision, audio files tend to be very large.

MIDI data, on the other hand, records the details of an instrumental performance digitally. When you play your MIDI keyboard into a Software Instrument track in GarageBand, data about each keypress is recorded, including the note's name, duration, and velocity (how hard you struck the note). But the sound of the music is played (or *rendered*) by your Mac using the specific Software Instrument you've assigned to that track.

For example, if you create a Software Instrument track using the Live Pop Horns preset, the music you record on that track will sound like horns. But you can change the track's instrument to something totally different, like Hollywood Strings, and the same notes you recorded will now sound like a string section.

The sounds for Software Instrument tracks are produced by taking a sound source, called a *generator*, and applying effects to it. In fact, you can design your own instruments by varying the preset effects settings for a generator (you'll learn about tweaking effects settings in Chapter 10). There are two classes of generators: sampled and synthesized.

Sampled sounds are based on samples, or recordings, taken from actual musical instruments. A set of samples usually includes recordings of many individual notes played on the instrument at different volumes and with a range of articulations. In general, the Software Instruments that are named after normal acoustic instruments use sampled generators.

Synthesized sounds are completely computer-generated and tend to sound artificial. These types of Software Instruments are based on synthesized generators: synthesizers, electric pianos, organs, and clavinets.

Software Instruments put a much greater strain on your computer than do Real Instruments, because GarageBand is creating the sound of each Software Instrument on the fly, in real time. To play a Real Instrument track, all the program has to do is read the recorded data from the hard disk and perhaps perform some effects processing. As a rule, the maximum number of Software Instrument tracks your Mac can handle in a GarageBand song is about half the number of Real Instrument tracks it can tolerate (see the sidebar "How Many Tracks Can I Use in My Song?" later in this chapter).

continues on next page

REAL VS. SOFTWARE INSTRUMENT TRACKS

Because MIDI files do not model the actual sound of a performance, they are smaller than audio files. They are also easily editable, because each note is recorded as a distinct unit of data. Compare **Figure 3.12** and **Figure 3.13**, which show, respectively, a Real Instrument track and a Software Instrument track as displayed in the track editor. Note the complexity of the audio file as depicted here. It's difficult to make out individual notes or find a pattern of beats. The MIDI file, however, is clarity itself. Each little rectangle represents a single note. The color of the rectangle shows the volume of the note, and the horizontal size of the rectangle shows the duration of the note. You can change any of these parameters in the track editor. You can even correct mistakes you made while playing! (You'll learn the details of working in the track editor in Chapter 9.)

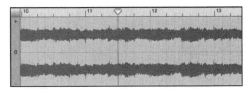

Figure 3.12 A region from a Real Instrument track, displayed in the track editor.

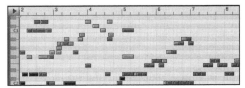

Figure 3.13 A region from a Software Instrument track, displayed in the track editor.

Figure 3.14 The Add Track button.

Figure 3.15 The New Track dialog.

Figure 3.16 Click the Real Instrument tab to choose an instrument preset for a Real Instrument track.

Adding a Real Instrument Track

When you create a Real Instrument track, the program asks you to choose an instrument for the track. This is more of a convenience than a necessity. GarageBand's Real Instruments are actually presets that include settings for effects, such as echo, reverb, and compression, that Apple thinks would enhance the instrument you're about to record. When you choose an instrument, you also get a lovely icon that helps to identify your track. You can always change any of these settings later, using the Track Info window (see "About the Track Info Window" later in this chapter).

To add a Real Instrument track:

1. *Do one of the following:*
   ▲ Choose Track > New Track (Command-Option-N).
   ▲ Click the Add Track button (**Figure 3.14**).

   The New Track dialog appears (**Figure 3.15**).

2. Click the Real Instrument tab, if it's not already selected (**Figure 3.16**).

continues on next page

ADDING A REAL INSTRUMENT TRACK

3. Select an instrument category in the left column; then, in the right column, select the specific instrument preset you want to use (**Figure 3.17**).

4. Choose a format by *doing one of the following*:

▲ If you've connected your instrument with a single mono cable (this is likely the case if you are recording an electric guitar, for example), or if you're recording through a single microphone, click the Format: Mono button (**Figure 3.18**). Then choose the correct channel from the Input popup menu (**Figure 3.19**). The number of channels listed on the menu will depend on your audio hardware (see Chapter 5 for more details on recording Real Instruments).

▲ If you're recording through a pair of stereo mikes (or some other stereo source), click the Format: Stereo button (**Figure 3.20**). Each item on the Input menu will now be a pair of channels (**Figure 3.21**). Choose one of these pairs from the menu.

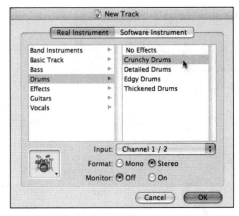

Figure 3.17 Choose a preset from the right column.

Figure 3.18 Choose the Mono format for your input.

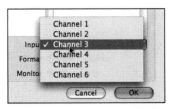

Figure 3.19 Select the Input channel.

Figure 3.20 Click the Stereo button.

Figure 3.21 Choose a pair of stereo input channels.

Figure 3.22 Click the On button to monitor your recording.

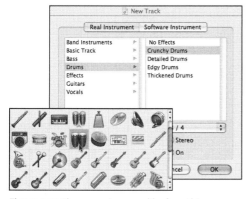

Figure 3.23 Choose an icon you like from this menu.

Figure 3.24 A new track appears in the timeline.

5. *Do one of the following:*

▲ To listen to your audio as it is being recorded, click the Monitor: On button (**Figure 3.22**).

▲ To prevent your audio from being played back through your Mac's speakers, click the Off button.

6. If you don't like the default icon for the instrument you've chosen, click the icon button and choose a new icon from the menu (**Figure 3.23**). (See "To change a track's instrument icon" later in this chapter.)

7. Click OK or press Return.

A new track is added to the timeline, below the other tracks (**Figure 3.24**).

✔ Tips

■ A new Real Instrument track is also created any time you drag a Real Instrument loop into the timeline (see Chapter 4). Likewise, if you drag an audio file into GarageBand from the Finder (see Chapter 12), it, too, is placed into a new track.

■ One thing you can't do with tracks is reorder them once they are created. If you care about the vertical arrangement of your tracks, plan it out ahead of time and add your tracks in the order you want.

About Basic Tracks

If you don't feel that you need GarageBand's assistance in setting up a track for recording a Real Instrument, you can skip the presets and fancy icons and start with a blank slate. To do this, you add a *basic* track to your song. This is a track with no effects applied (Echo and Reverb are enabled, but set to 0). You can adjust effects settings to your own liking and add an icon of your choice later, using the Track Info window (see "To change a track's instrument icon" at the end of this chapter; to adjust effects settings, see Chapter 10).

To add a basic track:

◆ *Do one of the following:*

▲ Choose Track > New Basic Track (**Figure 3.25**).

▲ Click the Add Track button or press Command-Option-N. The New Track dialog appears. Click the Real Instrument tab; then choose Basic Track in the left column and No Effects in the right column (**Figure 3.26**).

A new Real Instrument track appears below the other tracks in the timeline, bearing a generic icon and the name "No Effects" (**Figure 3.27**).

Figure 3.25 The New Basic Track command.

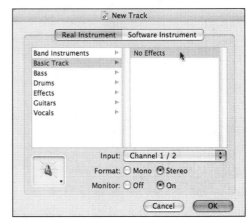

Figure 3.26 Choosing the preset for a new basic track.

Figure 3.27 The basic track takes its place in the timeline.

Figure 3.28 Click the Software Instrument tab at the top of the New Track dialog.

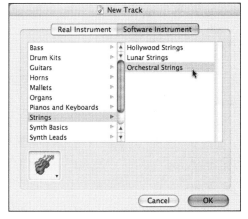

Figure 3.29 Choose a preset for the new track.

Adding a Software Instrument Track

The procedure for adding a Software Instrument track is very similar to that for adding a Real Instrument track. As with Real Instrument tracks, you are asked to assign an instrument to the track. Here the two procedures diverge. Whereas you can decline to choose an instrument for a Real Instrument track and opt for a basic track, with no effects applied, you have no such option with Software Instrument tracks. A Software Instrument track without an instrument would be silent! The instrument you choose for your new track defines the sound of the entire track.

Another difference is that you don't have to worry about telling the program what channels to use for input. Mac OS X handles the MIDI setup automatically in the background.

To add a Software Instrument track:

1. *Do one of the following:*
   ▲ Choose Track > New Track (Command-Option-N).
   ▲ Click the Add Track button (Figure 3.14).

   The New Track dialog appears (Figure 3.15).

2. Click the Software Instrument tab, if it's not already selected (**Figure 3.28**).

3. Select an instrument category in the left column; then, in the right column, select the specific instrument preset you want to use (**Figure 3.29**).

continues on next page

4. If you don't like the default icon for the instrument you've chosen, click the icon button and choose a new icon from the menu (**Figure 3.30**). (See "To change a track's instrument icon" later in this chapter.)

5. Click OK or press Return.

A new track is added to the timeline, below the other tracks (**Figure 3.31**).

✔ Tips

■ A new Software Instrument track is also created any time you drag a Software Instrument loop into the timeline (see Chapter 4).

■ One thing you can't do with tracks is reorder them once they are created. If you care about the vertical arrangement of your tracks, plan it out ahead of time and add your tracks in the order you want.

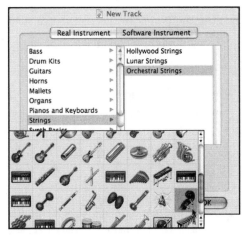

Figure 3.30 Choose a new icon for the track, if you like.

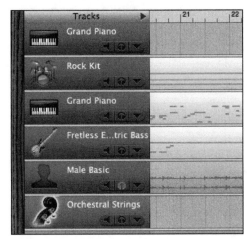

Figure 3.31 A brand-new Software Instrument track appears in the timeline.

ADDING A SOFTWARE INSTRUMENT TRACK

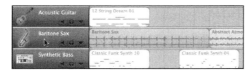

Figure 3.32 The Baritone Sax track is marked for oblivion.

Figure 3.33 The Baritone Sax track has been deleted, and the track below it has moved up to take its place.

Deleting Tracks

Sometimes you need to thin out the texture of your song by getting rid of a track or two. Fortunately, track deletion is undo-able.

To delete a track:

1. Select the track you wish to delete (**Figure 3.32**).

2. Choose Track > Delete Track or press Command-Delete.

   The track is removed from the timeline (**Figure 3.33**).

✔ Tips

- If you press the Delete key by itself, all regions will be deleted from the track, but the track itself will stay put. This operation is also undo-able.

- If you delete a track from the middle of the stack, the tracks below it move up to fill the gap.

About the Track Info Window

If you want to change the basic characteristics of a track after you've created it, the Track Info window is the place to do it (**Figure 3.34**). It's almost identical to the New Track dialog, with a few significant differences. Also, there are separate versions of the Track Info window for Real and Software Instruments, so you can't convert a Real Instrument track into a Software Instrument track, or vice versa.

The Track Info window is used primarily for changing the instrument (or the instrument icon) assigned to a track. You can't change the track's name here; to do that, you need to use the track editor (see Chapter 9). You can also change the recording settings for Real Instrument tracks; the Track Info window includes the same Input, Format, and Monitor recording controls as the New Track dialog, and they work identically (see "To add a Real Instrument track" earlier in this chapter).

Both flavors of the Track Info window include an extra widget in the lower-left corner that's not in the New Track dialog: the Details triangle. Clicking this triangle opens a new pane, which displays the effects settings for the selected track (**Figure 3.35**). I'll save the discussion of effects for Chapter 10.

You also use the Track Info window to alter the basic parameters of the song as a whole, by means of the song's master track, but that subject belongs in Chapter 11.

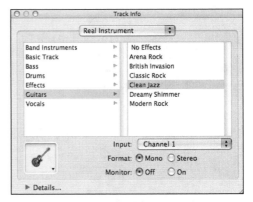

Figure 3.34 The Track Info window for a Real Instrument track.

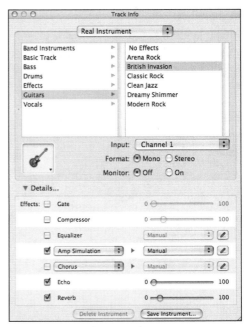

Figure 3.35 The Details pane of a Real Instrument Track Info window.

Figure 3.36 Click the Track Info button with a track selected. The track in this example is a Software Instrument track.

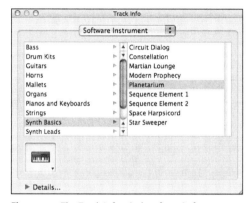

Figure 3.37 The Track Info window for a Software Instrument track.

To view the Track Info for a track:

◆ *Do one of the following:*

▲ Select the track header and click the Track Info button (**Figure 3.36**) or press Command-I.

▲ Double-click the track header.

The Track Info window opens (**Figure 3.37**).

✔ Tip

■ Note that the main part of the Track Info window for Real Instruments (Figure 3.34) is almost identical to that for Software Instruments (Figure 3.37). The only difference is the absence of recording options in the Software Instrument window.

Changing a Track's Instrument

Changing the instrument assigned to a track has very different consequences for Real and Software Instruments. As discussed earlier, a Real Instrument is just a collection of effects settings. Say that you create a Real Instrument track using the Solo Sax instrument and record a performance of a live saxophone player into it. If you switch the track's instrument to Pop Vocals, the basic instrumental sound of the track won't change. The effects that are part of the Pop Vocals preset will be applied to your recording, so its acoustical aura will change, but it will still sound like a saxophone.

Not so with Software Instruments. If you create a Software Instruments track using the Muted Electric Bass instrument and then change the track to something very different, like Synth Basics/Star Sweeper, the sound of the music recorded into the track will change completely. The notes will be the same; the dynamics and articulation will be the same, but the electric bass instrumental timbre will be gone and the synthesized sound will have taken its place.

To change a track's instrument:

1. Select the track whose instrument you want to change.

2. Open the Track Info window, using one of the techniques described in "To view the Track Info for a track" earlier in this chapter (**Figure 3.38**).

3. Select an instrument category in the left column; then, in the right column, select the specific instrument preset you want to use (**Figure 3.39**).

   You can leave the window open and try other instrument presets.

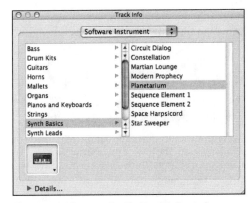

Figure 3.38 After opening the Track Info window.

Figure 3.39 Choosing a new category and instrument preset.

Figure 3.40 This dialog gives you an opportunity to save any changes you made to an instrument preset.

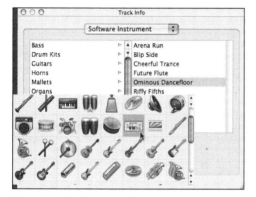

Figure 3.41 The instrument icon menu.

✔ Tip

■ If, before choosing a new instrument, you opened the Details pane of the Track Info window and made any changes (or so much as opened a single pop-up menu), you will see an alert dialog (**Figure 3.40**). If you don't want to save any changes to the current instrument, click Don't Save. The consequences of clicking Save are rather complex, so I will refer you to the sidebar "The Confusing 'Do You Want to Save' Dialog" in Chapter 10.

To change a track's instrument icon:

1. Select the track to which you wish to give a new icon.

2. Open the Track Info window.

3. Click the icon button.

   The icon menu appears (**Figure 3.41**).

4. Click the desired replacement icon to select it. Use the scroll bar, if necessary, to view the entire collection of icons.

✔ Tips

■ The icon menu can be tricky to work with. Click the icon button and then release the mouse button. The menu will stay open, and you can scroll through the whole set. If you change your mind and decide that you don't want to pick a new icon, just move the mouse away from the menu and click. The menu will close with no changes made.

■ Don't continue to press the mouse button after clicking the icon button. This makes it easier to inadvertently select a random icon and prevents you from using the scroll bar.

How Many Tracks Can I Use in My Song?

Each track you add to your song consumes a sizeable portion of your Mac's RAM, so try not to add unnecessary tracks. By default, GarageBand automatically limits the number of tracks available to you, taking into account the properties of your machine and the type of tracks you include in your song. The only way to find out what the limit is on your particular hardware is to bump into it by trying to add too many tracks. When you do, you'll get an alert (**Figure 3.42**), and GarageBand will refuse to carry out your last "New Track" command. On my 1 GHz G4 PowerBook, for example, with 1 GB of RAM, GarageBand maxes out at 16 Software Instrument tracks and 32 Real Instrument tracks.

GarageBand has your best interests at heart, of course, and is trying to help you keep the complexity of your songs to a level that your computer can handle. If you want to live dangerously and circumvent GarageBand's limits, you can change the Maximum Number of Tracks settings in GarageBand's Preferences.

1. Choose GarageBand > Preferences (Command-,). The Preferences dialog opens.

2. Click the Advanced button to display the Advanced pane (**Figure 3.43**). By default, the Maximum Number of Tracks is set to Automatic for both kinds of tracks.

3. Choose a new setting from the Real Instrument Tracks and/or Software Instrument Tracks pop-up menu. (**Figure 3.44**).

4. Close the dialog.

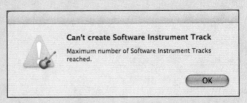

Figure 3.42 You've reached the maximum allowable Software Instrument tracks. The alert you see when you hit the limit of Real Instrument tracks is similar.

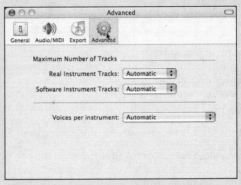

Figure 3.43 The Advanced pane of the GarageBand Preferences dialog.

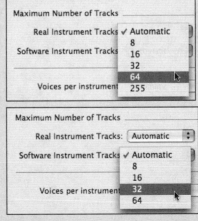

Figure 3.44 Setting the Maximum Number of Real Instrument tracks (top) and Software Instrument tracks (bottom).

CHANGING A TRACK'S INSTRUMENT

WORKING WITH LOOPS

Loops are short snippets of recorded music that are designed to fit together seamlessly. GarageBand ships with a large library of loops, so you can get started making music immediately, without the need for any special hardware other than your Mac.

In this chapter, you'll learn:

◆ What Apple Loops are and why they're so great.

◆ Several techniques for finding the perfect loop for your song among the thousand-or-so loops that are installed with GarageBand.

◆ How to audition loops before using them in your song.

◆ How to add Real Instrument and Software Instrument loops to your composition.

◆ How to add more loops to your library.

About Apple Loops

In general, loops are short, prerecorded pieces of music that are made so they fit smoothly together in sequence or so they can be repeated to make longer pieces of music.

What sets the Apple Loops that come with GarageBand apart from garden-variety loops is *metadata*. Metadata, here, is textual information that has been inserted into the file headers of Apple Loops. Without this metadata, a loop file would look like just an ordinary sound file to your computer. The metadata, however, includes loads of useful information about the sound file, such as the type of instruments recorded in the file, the style of the music in the file, and the music's key, tempo, and time signature.

The presence of this metadata adds enormously to the usefulness of Apple Loops. It means that if you decide you want a loop with a techno beat in A that lasts eight bars, you don't have to test every single loop in the program to find one. Instead, you can use powerful search features built into GarageBand to turn up just the right loop in a matter of seconds.

Another cool feature of Apple Loops is that they have markers attached to each beat. This means that you can add a loop to your song even if it was recorded at a different tempo. Its beat structure will adjust to your song's tempo without gaps or distortion.

GarageBand includes Apple Loops of both Real Instrument and Software Instrument types. You can add Real Instrument loops to Real Instrument tracks, and Software Instrument loops to tracks of either type. Once added to your song, both types of loops behave just like Real Instrument and Software Instrument material you recorded yourself.

About the Loop Browser

Sifting through the thousands of loops that come with GarageBand to find just the right one for your song can be an intimidating task. Fortunately, the program provides a nifty tool for the job: the loop browser (**Figure 4.1**).

The loop browser allows you to sort your loops using the keywords embedded in the Apple Loops installed with the program. You progressively narrow your search for specific loops based on three criteria:

◆ Genre (or style)

◆ Instrument

◆ Mood

The left part of the loop browser is taken up with the search interface, and the results of your search are displayed on the right, in a list that shows each loop's name, tempo, key, and length (in number of beats). Each loop is also identified by icon as a Real Instrument loop or a Software Instrument loop. You can also use the search results listing to mark frequently used loops as Favorites for quick access. And the loop browser lets you preview, or audition, loops so you can try them out with your song before deciding whether to use them.

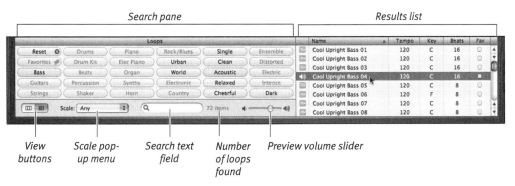

Search pane   Results list

View buttons   Scale pop-up menu   Search text field   Number of loops found   Preview volume slider

Figure 4.1 The loop browser.

ABOUT THE LOOP BROWSER

Displaying the Loop Browser

When you first start GarageBand, the loop browser is hidden to allow more room for tracks in the timeline, but it's easy to display.

Figure 4.2 The Loop Browser button.

To display the loop browser:

◆ If the loop browser is hidden, *do one of the following:*

▲ Click the Loop Browser button, near the bottom of the GarageBand window (**Figure 4.2**).

▲ Press Command-L.

The Loop Browser button glows blue, and the loop browser itself slides into view (**Figure 4.3**).

To hide the loop browser:

◆ Click the Loop Browser button or press Command-L.

The loop browser goes back into hiding.

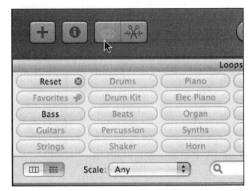

Figure 4.3 The loop browser appears.

Figure 4.4 The loop browser in button view.

Figure 4.5 The loop browser in column view.

Column view

Button view

Figure 4.6 The view buttons.

About the Loop Browser Views

The search pane (left side) of the loop browser has two viewing modes:

◆ Button view displays an array of buttons, each bearing a keyword (**Figure 4.4**).

◆ Column view sorts keywords using a three-column format resembling the Finder's column view (**Figure 4.5**).

Use the view buttons in the lower-left corner of the browser to choose a view (**Figure 4.6**).

Using Button View to Find Loops

In button view, you click keyword buttons to narrow the list of available loops. The first button you click brings up a long list of loops in the results list. Each succeeding button you click reduces the number of loops displayed. You can start with any button and click other buttons in any order, so button view encourages free-form searching. Note that as you click buttons, others become dimmed. This means there are no loops that share those two characteristics—there are no loops that share the keywords *Country* and *Strings*, for example.

To find loops using button view:

1. Click the button to switch to button view (Figure 4.6).

2. Click a keyword button that characterizes the kind of loop you're looking for (**Figure 4.7**).

   The button you clicked glows blue, and buttons with incompatible keywords are dimmed. A list of loops appears in the results pane of the loop browser (**Figure 4.8**). The number of loops in the list appears beneath the buttons.

3. You can choose a loop at any time from the results list, or you can continue to click buttons with keywords that describe your desired loop to narrow the search (**Figure 4.9**).

   Notice that the number of loops found shrinks with each button click.

4. Once the list of results produces the loop you want, add it to your song (see "Adding a Loop to Your Song" later in this chapter).

Figure 4.7 Preparing to click a keyword button.

Number of loops found

Figure 4.8 After clicking, the button is selected, and the results list shows loops described by the keyword.

Figure 4.9 Click more buttons to narrow your search.

Figure 4.10 Click the Reset button to start searching from scratch.

✔ Tips

■ To deactivate a button you have clicked, click it again. It returns to its original state.

■ To start a fresh search, click the Reset button to deselect all of the buttons you clicked in the course of the previous search (**Figure 4.10**).

Figure 4.11 The keyword contextual menu.

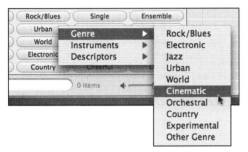

Figure 4.12 Navigate through the menu hierarchy and choose a new keyword.

Figure 4.13
The button, now graced with a different keyword.

Figure 4.14
Starting to drag the button to move it.

Figure 4.15
Poised over the new position.

Figure 4.16
The keywords swap places.

Customizing Button View

GarageBand's collection of Apple Loops contains more keywords than there are buttons in the loop browser. Indeed, to save space, the loop browser doesn't even ordinarily display all of its buttons at once, but you can expand the loop browser to see more buttons (see the sidebar "Expanding the Loop Browser to See More Buttons" later in this chapter). You can reassign keywords to buttons to make sure that the keywords you use most often are available. You can also arrange keywords in the order that works best for you. And if you make a mess of things, you can use GarageBand's Preferences dialog to put the keywords back in their original places.

To change the keyword on a button:

1. Control-click the button whose keyword you wish to replace (**Figure 4.11**).

   A contextual menu appears, listing all of the available keywords.

2. Choose a new keyword from the menu (**Figure 4.12**).

   The new keyword is assigned to the button (**Figure 4.13**).

To move a keyword to another button:

1. Drag the button whose keyword you wish to move over another button (**Figure 4.14**).

   When the button you're dragging is in the right position, the target button will darken (**Figure 4.15**).

2. Release the mouse button.

   The two keywords exchange places (**Figure 4.16**).

To restore keywords to their original locations:

1. Choose GarageBand > Preferences (Command-,) to open the Preferences dialog (**Figure 4.17**). If the General pane is not visible, click the General button.

2. Click the Keyword Layout: Reset button.

   A warning dialog appears, asking whether you're sure that you want to continue (**Figure 4.18**).

3. *Do one of the following:*

   ▲ Click Yes to continue. The keywords will be reset to their original configuration.

   ▲ Click No to cancel the operation. The keywords will be left as they are.

4. Click the close button (Command-W) in the Preferences dialog to close it.

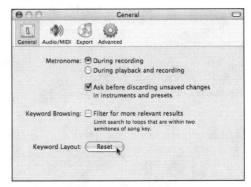

Figure 4.17 The GarageBand Preferences dialog, showing the General pane.

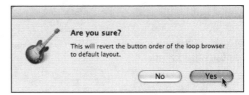

Figure 4.18 One last chance to make up your mind.

Expanding the Loop Browser to See More Buttons

Not only does the loop browser have fewer buttons than keywords, it doesn't even display all of the buttons it has when you first open it. By default, 30 buttons are shown (including the Reset and Favorites buttons), but the complete loop browser holds 54 buttons.

Here's how to see them all:

1. Move the mouse pointer to the area that divides the timeline from the loop browser. Stay to the left of the Record button or to the right of the time display. The pointer changes into a hand (**Figure 4.19**).

2. Drag upward to reveal more rows of buttons. You can display up to nine rows (**Figure 4.20**).

   If you stop dragging while a row is partially visible, the browser will snap to the next complete row.

Figure 4.19 Position the mouse pointer above the loop browser.

Figure 4.20 When you drag upward, more buttons are revealed.

Using Column View to Find Loops

Column view provides a more guided approach to searching for loops. The first column shows the three general keyword types (plus All and Favorites). The columns at the right narrow down the list of keywords, and clicking an item in the rightmost column results in a list of loops.

To find loops using column view:

1. Click the button to switch to column view (Figure 4.6).

2. Click a keyword type in the left column (headed "Loops") to select it (**Figure 4.21**).

   The type you selected in the left column becomes the heading of the middle column, which displays the categories available within that type (**Figure 4.22**).

3. Click one of the categories in the middle column to select it.

   The item you selected becomes the heading for the third column, which lists the keywords available within that category (**Figure 4.23**).

4. Click one of the keywords in the third column to see a list of loops that satisfy the criteria you selected in the second and third columns. The number in parentheses indicates the number of loops that will be listed (**Figure 4.24**).

   The loops that have made it through the sorting process appear in the results list.

Figure 4.21 Click one of the types in the left column.

Figure 4.22 The categories within that keyword type appear in the second column.

Figure 4.23 Select a category to see a list of keywords.

Figure 4.24 Finally, click a keyword to generate a list of matching loops.

✔ Tip

■ To see a broader range of loops in the results list, you can select multiple keywords in the third column. Shift-click two keywords in the list to select a range of keywords, or Command-click to select noncontiguous keywords. Apple's documentation says that you can also select multiple categories in the second column, but that doesn't seem to work in the shipping software.

Having Trouble Finding Loops?

When you open the loop browser, you sometimes may find many of the buttons dimmed even before you start sorting. Or in column view, when you click a category in the second column, nothing may show up in the third column.

There are two possible causes:

- ◆ GarageBand may be hiding loops whose original keys are far removed from the key of your song. Although the program can transpose any loop to your song's key, not all such key shifts are desirable. For example, if your song is in D and you add a trumpet loop that was originally in A, the loop has to be transposed downward seven semitones. The loop will not only change pitch, but will also change substantially in color. It may not even sound much like a trumpet any more!

    By default, GarageBand is set to show you only loops whose original keys are within two semitones (a whole step) of the song's key. If you want to turn off this protective behavior, you need to visit GarageBand > Preferences (Command-,) and click the General button. Uncheck the box next to Keyword Browsing: Filter for More Relevant Results (**Figure 4.25**). Now GarageBand won't restrict your loop browsing based on key.

- ◆ If your song uses a time signature other than 4/4, very few loops will show up in the loop browser. Indeed, if you choose one of the more exotic time signatures, like 5/4 or even 2/2, you may see no loops at all. The situation improves somewhat if you purchase and install the supplemental GarageBand Jam Pack. Among the thousands of loops it adds to your library, a few are in these unusual time signatures, but for now, if you plan to do a lot of composition with loops in GarageBand, stick to 4/4.

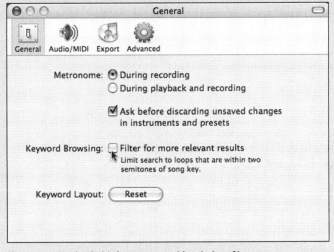

Figure 4.25 Uncheck this box to get a wider choice of loops.

Finding Loops by Other Methods

GarageBand allows you to augment your search for the perfect loop with a few auxiliary techniques. You can search for loops with specific text in the name or path (the categories and keywords GarageBand uses to classify loops). Or you can look for loops that are compatible with certain types of scales (major, minor, neither, or both) to narrow the list to loops that are more compatible with the scale your song uses.

You can use either of these methods instead of the button and column search methods or to further refine the results you get from those techniques.

To find loops by using a text search:

◆ Type the text you are looking for into the search field (identified by the magnifying glass icon) at the bottom of the loop browser and press Return (**Figure 4.26**).

Loops whose name or path includes the search text will appear in the results list (**Figure 4.27**).

✔ Tip

■ To clear the search field, click the *x* icon at the right side of the field.

To find loops by scale type:

◆ Choose the type of scale you prefer from the Scale pop-up menu at the bottom of the loop browser (**Figure 4.28**).

Loops that do not match the selected scale type will be removed from the results list.

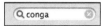

Figure 4.26 Type search text in this field.

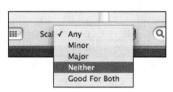

Click here to clear the search text field

Figure 4.27 Matching loops appear in the list.

Figure 4.28 The Scale pop-up menu.

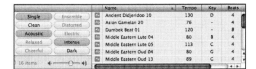

Figure 4.29 The results list.

Working with the Results List

Whether you use the button view or the column view to sort GarageBand's loops, the loops that make it through the winnowing process are listed in the results list, at the right side of the loop browser (**Figure 4.29**). The number of loops in the list is shown to the right of the text search field.

By default, the loops found are listed alphabetically by name. Other columns show the original tempo and key and the length, measured in beats, for each loop. There's also a check box that allows you to designate loops you like as "favorites." Each listing includes an icon that distinguishes Real Instrument loops (a blue waveform) from Software Instrument loops (a green eighth note). You can re-sort this list using any of the columns and invert any column's sorting order.

If you want to listen to a loop before plopping it into your song, click its name in the list. And when you're ready to add a loop to your composition, you drag it from this list into the timeline.

Sorting the Results List

By default, the loops in the results list are sorted by name, but you can also sort the list on any of the other columns as well:

◆ Tempo

◆ Key

◆ Beats (length)

◆ Fav (whether the loop has been marked as a favorite)

You can also change the sort order for any column. The sort order is indicated by a tiny triangle at the right side of the header of the active column. If the point is on top, the column will sort in ascending order. If the triangle points downward, the column will sort in descending order.

To sort the results list:

◆ Click the heading of the column on which you want to sort the list (**Figure 4.30**).

GarageBand re-sorts the list (**Figure 4.31**).

To change the sort order of a column:

◆ Click the header of the currently active column (Figure 4.31).

The column's sort order is inverted (**Figure 4.32**).

Figure 4.30 Clicking the Tempo column header to re-sort the list.

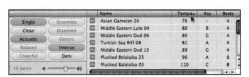

Figure 4.31 The list is now sorted by tempo, in ascending order.

Figure 4.32 After you click the Tempo header again, the list is sorted in descending order.

	Name ▲	Tempo	Key	Beats	Fav
	80s Rock Guitar 01	121	G	8	☐
◀	Acoustic Noodling 01	120	A	16	
	Acoustic Noodling 02	106	C	8	

Figure 4.33 Click this box to mark the loop as a favorite.

	Name ▲	Tempo	Key	Beats	Fav
	80s Rock Guitar 01	121	G	8	☐
◀	Acoustic Noodling 01	120	A	16	
	Acoustic Noodling 02	106	C	8	

Figure 4.34 Now the loop will appear in the Favorites category.

Figure 4.35 The Favorites button.

	Name ▲	Tempo	Key	Beats	Fav
	70s Ballad Piano 02	80	C	16	☑
	80s Pop Beat 07	110	–	8	☑
	Acoustic Noodling 01	120	A	16	☑
	Acoustic Picking 06	90	D	16	☑
	Blue Jazz Organ Riff 02	136	C	16	☑
	Funky Electric Guitar 06	90	C	8	☑

Figure 4.36 Your favorite loops are listed.

Marking Loops as Favorites

If you find yourself using certain loops over and over again, you can save yourself the trouble of searching for them each time by declaring them as *favorites*. Each favorite loop has its own keyword that brings the loop to the surface quickly when you're browsing in either button view or column view. These favorites are not song specific—they'll show up as favorites in every song you work on in GarageBand.

To mark a loop as a favorite:

◆ Find the loop and make sure it is visible in the results list. Click the loop's check box in the Fav column (**Figure 4.33**). A check appears in the box (**Figure 4.34**).

To find favorite loops in button view:

◆ Make sure button view is active; then click the Favorites button (**Figure 4.35**). The loops you have marked as favorites appear in the results list (**Figure 4.36**).

✔ Tip

■ The Favorites button is available only if you have marked some loops as favorites. Otherwise, it's dimmed.

To find favorite loops in column view:

1. Make sure the loop browser is displayed in column view; then click Favorites in the Loops column.

   A list of the keyword categories that include favorite loops appears in the second column (**Figure 4.37**).

2. Click a category in the Favorites column.

   A list of the keywords associated with favorite loops appears in the third column (**Figure 4.38**).

3. Click a keyword in the third column.

   The loops associated with that keyword appear in the results list (**Figure 4.39**).

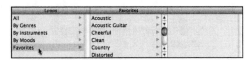

Figure 4.37 Clicking Favorites in the first column displays categories that contain favorite loops.

Figure 4.38 Clicking one of these categories generates a list of keywords.

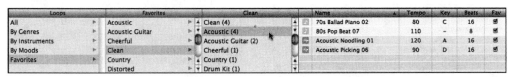

Figure 4.39 Click a keyword to see a list of favorite loops that fall under that keyword.

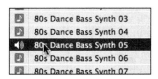

Figure 4.40 Click the loop in the results list to listen to it.

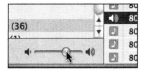

Figure 4.41 Drag the slider to adjust playback volume.

Auditioning Loops

As The Bard said, "What's in a name?" You can't tell if a loop is right for you just from its name; you need to listen to it. Once loops appear in the results list, you can click them to hear how they sound. Apple calls this *previewing* a loop, but that seems an odd word to use for a nonvisual activity; *audition* seems like a more appropriate word.

You can audition a loop by itself or try it with the song playing in the background. No matter what tempo and key are given for a loop in the results list, they will always match the tempo and key of the song when you audition it.

To audition a loop in the loop browser:

1. Click the loop's name in the results list (**Figure 4.40**).

   The loop will start to play, and its icon will change to a loudspeaker. The loop's tempo and key will be synchronized with those of the song.

2. To adjust the playback volume of the loop, drag the volume slider in the loop browser (**Figure 4.41**).

3. To stop playback, click the loop's listing again.

✔ Tip

■ If you change a loop's volume while auditioning it and then drag the loop to a new track in the timeline, that track inherits the loop's volume setting. If you drag it to an existing track, the loop uses the volume setting of the existing track.

Adding a Loop to Your Song

Once you've found a loop you like, you can add it to your song's timeline by dragging it from the list produced by your search. The left edge of the loop snaps to the nearest downbeat (the first beat of a measure). Alternatively, you can drag a loop to the track header, and GarageBand will place the loop at the beginning of the song.

You can drag the loop to a pre-existing track of the appropriate kind, or you can create a new track. Adding a loop to the timeline creates a region from the loop. Any changes you make to the region do not affect the original loop (see Chapter 8 to learn about editing regions). The tempo and key of this new region automatically adapt to the tempo and key of the song.

Real Instrument loops can be placed only in Real Instrument tracks. Software Instrument loops, on the other hand, can be placed in tracks of either type; however, if you drag a Software Instrument loop to a Real Instrument track, GarageBand converts it to a Real Instrument region.

To add a loop to your song while creating a new track:

1. Drag a loop of either type to the blank area of the timeline (**Figure 4.42**).

   As your pointer enters the timeline, a gray vertical bar appears, indicating the downbeat where the start of the loop will be placed.

2. Release the mouse button when you find the right spot.

   A new track is created below the pre-existing tracks (**Figure 4.43**). It's of the same type (Real or Software Instrument) as the loop, and it takes its instrument, icon, effect, and input settings from the loop as well.

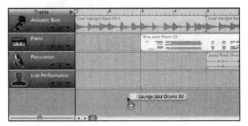

Figure 4.42 Dragging a loop to the timeline.

Figure 4.43 A new track is added to the song.

Figure 4.44 The green icon shows you that you're in the right place.

Figure 4.45 A plain icon shows you that you're in the wrong neighborhood.

To add a loop to a pre-existing track:

1. *Do one of the following:*
   ▲ Drag a Real Instrument loop to a Real Instrument track.
   ▲ Drag a Software Instrument loop to a track of either type.

   If you are dragging the loop over the correct type of track, the pointer will have a green plus (+) icon attached (**Figure 4.44**), and a gray vertical bar will appear, indicating the downbeat where the start of the loop will be placed. If these items are missing, you're over the wrong kind of track (**Figure 4.45**).

2. When you find the right location for the loop, release the mouse button to add the loop to the track.

   The loop will snap to the location of the vertical gray bar.

Region Names

When you drag a Real Instrument loop to the timeline and drop it into place, a new region is created. Each new region is named after the loop that it's derived from, with a numerical suffix appended.

The first time you drag Blip Synth 01 into your song, for example, the region added to the target track is named Blip Synth 01.1. If you add the same loop to your song again, the resulting region will be Blip Synth 01.2 (**Figure 4.46**). Names of additional instances of the same loop will continue to be incremented by 0.1. The same thing happens if you copy a region and paste it into a song: the name of the pasted region will be incremented by 0.1.

Software Instrument loops that are dragged into Real Instrument tracks receive the same treatment; they are, after all, turned into Real Instrument regions by the action (**Figure 4.47**). This is not true for Software Instruments added to Software Instrument tracks; all instances of Software Instrument regions have the same name (**Figure 4.48**).

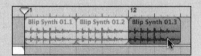

Figure 4.46 Each time the same loop is added to a Real Instrument track, the name of the resulting region is incremented by 0.1.

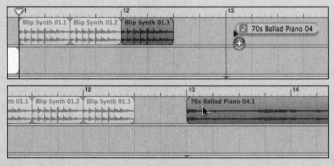

Figure 4.47 Software Instruments become Real Instrument regions.

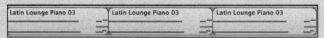

Figure 4.48 All instances of Software Instrument regions have the same name.

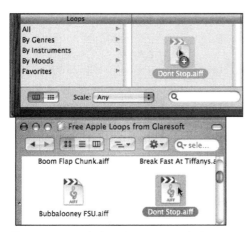

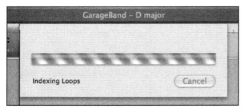

Figure 4.49 Drag the loop file's icon into the loop browser.

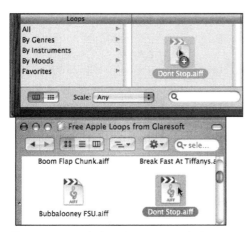

Figure 4.50 GarageBand may take several minutes to finish the process of copying and indexing the added loops.

Adding More Loops to GarageBand

In large part due to the popularity of GarageBand, the supply of Apple Loops is growing rapidly. GarageBand can also use any loops made for Soundtrack. You can add individual loop files to GarageBand or a whole folder full at once. Keep in mind that if you want to import loops from non-Apple sources into GarageBand, you'll need to convert them to the Apple Loop format with the Soundtrack Loop Utility (see the sidebar "Creating Your Own Loops").

To add loops to GarageBand:

1. Make sure that the Finder icon for the loop file (or folder of loops) is visible.

2. Drag the file (or folder) icon into the loop browser (**Figure 4.49**).

   GarageBand will copy the loops into the Apple Loops library and add the information about the loops to the index (**Figure 4.50**).

Creating Your Own Loops

If you feel adventurous and want to try your hand at making your own loops, you can use Apple's Soundtrack Loop Utility (SLU) to convert any AIFF or WAV file into an Apple Loop. SLU is bundled with the Soundtrack application, but if you don't own that program, you can get SLU from Apple free of charge. Download the Apple Loops SDK from ftp://ftp.apple.com/developer/Development_Kits/.

Run the installer contained in the downloaded file, and it will put the Soundtrack Loop Utility in your /Applications/Utilities folder. The installer will also place some thorough documentation in /Developer/Apple Loops SDK.

You'll find an excellent tutorial on using the Soundtrack Loop Utility at maczealots.com/tutorials/loops/.

HARDWARE FOR RECORDING

5

If you want to go beyond composing with Apple Loops and include original material in your songs, sooner or later you'll have to deal with hardware. It's certainly possible to sink a lot of money into creating a first-class recording studio, but it's not necessary. You can have a lot of fun creating music with GarageBand, and produce fine-sounding results, with a modest outlay of your hard-earned cash.

This chapter doesn't attempt to cover the universe of music hardware in encyclopedic fashion. I describe the general types of equipment available and then zero in on specific features that are of use to GarageBand artists. In the course of the chapter, you'll learn about:

◆ Hardware for recording audio.

◆ The different types of microphones.

◆ What to look for in a computer audio interface.

◆ Hardware for recording MIDI data.

◆ MIDI controllers.

◆ What to look for in a MIDI keyboard.

◆ What to look for in a MIDI interface.

HARDWARE FOR RECORDING

About Hardware

Audio recording (for Real Instrument tracks) is completely different, technically speaking, from recording MIDI data (for Software Instruments), and in the past, you needed separate equipment for each. Nowadays, with the continuing advances in the miniaturization of electronic circuitry, you can find some components that can be used for both tasks.

Apple-Certified Hardware

In the GarageBand Support area of its Web site, Apple posts a list of compatible devices. The list includes audio and/or MIDI interfaces, USB keyboards, and speakers, with links to manufacturers' Web pages. Now, there's nothing on the page that says how these products were chosen, or how rigorous the evaluation procedure was, or what criteria had to be met for an item to be included. The one thing all of the devices have in common is that you can buy them through the Apple Store. Nevertheless, if you're thinking about adding some music hardware to your system to use with GarageBand, it's certainly worth checking out the specifications and features of the equipment listed on this page:

www.apple.com/ilife/garageband/
compatibility.html

Hardware for Recording Audio

The hardware requirements for computer-based audio recording can be boiled down to two fundamental items:

◆ An audio source

◆ An audio interface

The audio source can take any of a number of forms; it can be an electric guitar (or any guitar with a pickup), or a microphone in front of a singer, or an electronic keyboard. The audio source takes the sound produced by the singer or instrument and converts it to an electronic signal. The signal is still in analog form, however, and for the computer to be able to record the sound, the signal has to be translated into digital information that the computer can understand. That's where the audio interface comes in. It's a piece of hardware that converts the original analog sound wave into digits. This component can be either inside your Mac or in a box connected to your Mac via a USB or FireWire cable.

Most modern Macintoshes come with some kind of hardware for digitizing analog audio built in as standard equipment. If you have one of these machines, you can use a $1/4$-inch-to-miniplug adapter cable (available for a few dollars at any electronics store) to plug your electric guitar directly into your Mac's audio-in port. That's about the simplest recording setup imaginable. But if you don't have an electric guitar, or if you want more flexibility or higher quality, there are many other options available to you.

continues on next page

I'm going to restrict my discussion to equipment at the modest end of the spectrum, both in terms of features and cost. I figure that if people are using a $49 music program, they probably don't have thousands of dollars budgeted for music hardware. Not only that, but GarageBand has some inherent limitations that put a damper on the usefulness of elaborate audio gadgets. Principal among these is the fact that GarageBand can record only a single mono track or one pair of stereo tracks at a time—in other words, no fancy multitrack recording allowed. (One way of getting around this constraint is to use a mixer. See the sidebar "Recording Multiple Sources at Once in GarageBand.") Therefore, spending hundreds of dollars on a 32-track audio interface with eight analog inputs would be pointless, at least for use exclusively with GarageBand.

Recording Multiple Sources at Once in GarageBand

How can you get around the one-track recording limitation of GarageBand? What if you're recording a large ensemble and want to use multiple microphones? Or what if you're recording a group with several electronic instruments? GarageBand can deal with only one of those instruments at a time.

One answer is to use a *mixer*. A mixer is an electronic device that can accept audio from more than one input simultaneously and combine the signals into a single output (or two stereo outputs). Mixers also usually have controls for each input, called *faders*, that let you set individual levels for each input, so you can achieve just the right balance between your cousin's delicate Celtic harp and your overbearing brother-in-law's obnoxious tuba.

Plug the output from the mixer into your audio interface, and GarageBand will see the entire group as a single input and record them all into one track.

Audio Sources

Audio sources fall into two general categories:

- Performer and microphone
- Instrument with electronic audio output

Microphones

For recording musical instruments that don't have an audio-out port (such as acoustic guitars, saxophones, percussion instruments, and human beings), a microphone is indispensable. A really good microphone will make a significant difference in the quality of your recording. Even if you're assembling the rest of your studio on a shoestring, buy the best mike you can possibly afford.

Keep in mind that a microphone puts out a tiny signal, much smaller than that produced by electronic instruments like guitars and synthesizers. You need to plug the mike into another component called a *pre-amplifier*, or *pre-amp* for short. This boosts the microphone's output to the same level as the output from a guitar or synthesizer, which is called a *line-level* signal. Pre-amps are often separate units, but some mixers and audio interfaces have pre-amps integrated into them.

There is great variety among microphones, not only in terms of quality and fidelity of music reproduction, but also in terms of suitability to task. For example, some mikes are great for voices in live performance, and some work better for recording voices in the studio. Some are good for capturing the nuances of acoustic guitar sound, but are overwhelmed by the violent attack of a drumstick on a cymbal.

continues on next page

AUDIO SOURCES

Microphones use an extremely thin membrane called a *diaphragm* (usually made of plastic or Mylar) to pick up sound waves in the air. The resulting vibrations of the diaphragm are converted to electrical impulses by a mechanism called a *transducer*. Microphones are commonly classified according to the type of transducer they incorporate. The two most common types of transducer in use today are *dynamic* and *condenser*.

♦ **Dynamic:** In dynamic microphones, the diaphragm is attached to an object that conducts electricity, like a coil of wire. This coil is suspended between two magnets, so that when the diaphragm (with its attached coil) vibrates in response to a sound wave, an electric current flows through the coil.

Dynamic mikes are resilient and are good at handling high sound pressure levels (SPLs). You'll often find them onstage in rock concerts, because they can handle loud percussion attacks, hard-driven guitar amps, and equally hard-driving vocalists. They also stand up to physical abuse well.

As you might guess from the preceding description, dynamic mikes aren't terribly subtle in terms of sonic reproduction. They produce a sound that is sometimes called "gritty" rather than warm and nuanced.

♦ **Condenser:** A condenser microphone's diaphragm is suspended in front of a metal plate, and a constant voltage is applied across the gap, creating an electric field. Sound waves cause the diaphragm to vibrate, producing ripples in the field, which, in turn, cause a current to flow.

Figure 5.1 A condenser microphone.

The diaphragms in condenser mikes have less mass than those in dynamic mikes and so are more easily moved by sound waves. As a result, condenser mikes are better at picking up the fine details of a sound and are more sensitive to high frequencies. Because condenser microphones more faithfully reproduce the original sounds, they tend to be popular in recording studios (**Figure 5.1**).

On the other hand, their greater sensitivity can make them tricky to work with, because they're not only sensitive to the subtleties of music, but also to stray noises that may afflict your recording session. They're also more fragile than dynamic mikes—you don't want your performers bumping into them.

One last point: condenser mikes need a constant source of juice to maintain that electrical field. Most mikes can be battery powered, but batteries always run out just when you need them most. Many mikes will also run on *phantom power*, which is supplied through the microphone cable by some pre-amps, mixers, and audio interfaces.

Other audio sources

By "other audio sources," I mean electronic instruments that have audio-out ports.

Digital pianos and other electronic keyboards fit into this category. You can also buy electric pickups for violins, cellos, mandolins, and other stringed instruments. But the most common electronic instrument is the electric guitar or bass. To record an electric guitar in GarageBand, simply unplug the guitar from its amp and then plug that same cable into an audio interface. GarageBand's Real Instruments include effects settings that reproduce several types of guitar amp, so you have a wider range of sound available than if you used just your physical amp.

Audio Interfaces

An audio interface performs one basic function: it converts the analog signal from your audio source to a digital signal your computer can understand. The audio interface receives the analog signal either from your pre-amp or by direct input from an electronic instrument such as an electric guitar or synthesizer.

Choosing an audio interface

At the core of any audio interface is the *analog-digital converter*, or *ADC*. This is the circuitry that does the heavy lifting of sampling the audio waveform many times per millisecond and converting the results to numbers. The more often it samples the wave, the more accurately the numbers it comes up with describe the original sound. The number of times the ADC samples the wave each second is referred to as the *sampling rate* and is expressed as a frequency, in kilohertz (thousands of samples per second), abbreviated kHz.

It's also important to know the ADC's maximum *resolution*. This tells you how precisely the ADC measures the sound wave while taking each sample. Resolution is described in terms of the number of binary digits, or *bits*, in the resulting measurement; 24-bit resolution, for example, is more precise than 16-bit resolution.

Which Macs Have Audio-In Ports?

In April 2002, after a long period of absence, audio-in ports began to re-appear on Apple's professional computers (and the eMac). The first iMacs included them in February 2003, and by September all iMac models had audio-in ports. Alas, iBooks have always been free of audio-in hardware.

Recent models with audio-digitizing hardware include the following:

PowerBooks

- PowerBook G4 (DVI)
- PowerBook G4 (1 GHz/867 MHz)
- PowerBook G4 (12.1")
- PowerBook G4 (17")
- PowerBook G4 (12.1" DVI)
- PowerBook G4 (15" FireWire 800)
- PowerBook G4 (17" 1.33 GHz)

Desktop Macs

- Power Macintosh G4 (Mirrored Drive Doors)
- Power Macintosh G4 (FireWire 800)
- Power Macintosh G5

iMacs

- iMac (early 2003) (1 GHz model only)
- iMac (USB 2.0)

All eMac models

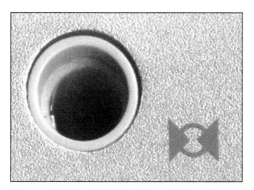

Figure 5.2 This icon identifies the audio-in port on your Macintosh.

Built-in audio

As mentioned earlier, most recent Macs have audio digitizing capability built in (**Figure 5.2**). This built-in audio hardware is certainly convenient, but it has its limitations. First, the ADCs built into current Macintosh systems max out at 16-bit resolution. This is adequate for basic recording purposes—for instance, to digitize an old LP or cassette that you plan to burn to CD or convert to MP3 and store in iTunes. It's also just barely adequate for GarageBand, because GarageBand supports only 16-bit recording. But this hardware doesn't leave you any headroom, nor will it be able to grow with you when your needs change in the future. Second, the audio connector on these Macs accepts a line-level connection, meaning that you can't hook up a microphone directly to your computer. You need to connect it to a pre-amp or mixer first.

Third, the audio-in ports on these Macs use 1/8-inch connectors, called *mini-jacks*, which do not provide top quality. Tiny connectors like these, which may be fine for Walkman headphones, are inadequate for truly high-quality signal transmission. Most of the components used for audio recording employ somewhat more substantial connectors and cables, which impede current flow less and provide more shielding from outside sources of interference. To connect your instrument, mixer, or pre-amp to one of these mini-jacks, you need an adapter, and adapters degrade signal quality as well.

When choosing a third-party audio interface, the first decision is: internal or external?

Internal interfaces

Internal interfaces (also called *soundcards*) are installed either in a PCI slot in desktop machines (**Figure 5.3**) or, less commonly, in the PCMCIA/CardBus slot of a laptop. This arrangement saves you some space on your desk (and in your laptop bag), but has some disadvantages. The inside of your computer is a noisy place, electronically speaking, and internal audio interfaces are subject to interference from the other components inside the machine. Plus, soundcards communicate with the outside world only through a narrow slot in the side of your Mac, which doesn't leave room for large, high-quality audio connectors.

Further, it's hard to share a soundcard among multiple computers. If you like to do some of your recording on a desktop Mac at home, but you also like to use your PowerBook as the hub of a portable studio while you're on the road, an external audio interface is probably what you're looking for.

External interfaces

An external audio interface is basically a box containing the same circuitry as an internal audio interface. Confusingly, you will find that many people use the term *soundcard* for this piece of equipment, just because the legacy of internal audio hardware is so strong. Because an external enclosure has more elbow room than a PCI slot, external audio interfaces often sport more rugged connectors (and more of them) than do soundcards (**Figure 5.4**).

Once upon a time, external audio interfaces required that you install an accompanying proprietary card in your computer to mediate between the two devices. Nowadays, external audio interfaces connect to your Mac by means of either USB or FireWire.

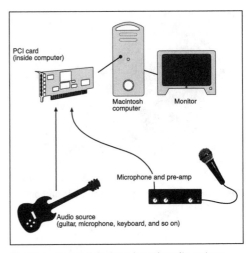

Figure 5.3 A typical desktop-based studio, using a PCI-slot audio interface.

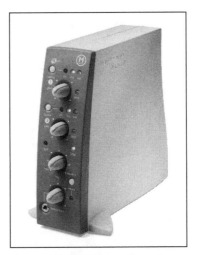

Figure 5.4 The Digidesign Mbox, a bus-powered USB audio interface with two analog inputs, two microphone pre-amps, phantom power, two analog outputs, 24-bit resolution, and more. (Photo courtesy of Digidesign.)

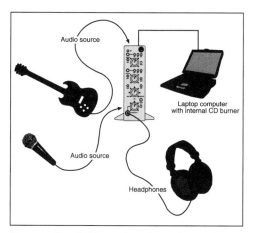

Audio source

Laptop computer
with internal CD burner

Audio source

Headphones

Figure 5.5 A typical laptop-based recording studio, using a USB-connected audio interface incorporating a microphone pre-amp.

- ◆ **USB:** The USB (for Universal Serial Bus) standard was originally designed for connecting computers to humdrum peripherals like keyboards (of the QWERTY variety) and mice and as a consequence supports only a relatively low data rate. But it turns out that that data rate is just sufficient to carry one or two tracks of digitized audio—perfect for GarageBand (**Figure 5.5**).

- ◆ **FireWire:** Apple originally developed the FireWire bus standard (also known as IEEE 1394b) to provide a high-bandwidth data path for connecting hard drives to computers. With a throughput about 40 or 50 times the rate of USB, audio interfaces that connect via FireWire can easily handle multiple tracks of recorded data simultaneously. But since GarageBand can't, a FireWire audio interface is probably more than you need.

Features to look for in audio recording equipment

Audio equipment marketing materials emphasize long lists of features. Here are a few features that you'll actually find to be useful in either internal or external interfaces:

- ◆ **24-bit/96 KHz:** An ADC that digitizes audio with a sampling rate of 44.1 kHz at 16-bit resolution will do just fine for compact discs and GarageBand, but that leaves you very little headroom for processing. The newly emerging standard for digital audio uses 24-bit resolution and a 96-kHz sampling rate for greater fidelity, dynamic range (the difference between the loudest and softest sounds), and signal-to-noise ratio. If you're serious enough about recording to buy a new audio interface, get one with a 24-bit/96Khz ADC, so whenever you're ready to graduate to

continues on next page

more sophisticated software, your equipment won't hold you back.

◆ **Microphone pre-amps:** If your audio interface incorporates microphone pre-amps, that will save you having to buy, store, and schlep around a separate box. And as long as you're looking for an interface with pre-amps, check to see whether it has phantom power, too, to keep your condenser mikes running happily without batteries. Because of space constraints, it's rare to find pre-amps in an internal interface.

◆ **Bus power:** Both USB and FireWire buses carry a little extra current along with the data stream, which can be used to provide connected devices with power. This can save you from having to lug around yet one more item of equipment: the power brick.

◆ **MIDI connectors:** If you plan to record to both Real and Software Instrument tracks in your GarageBand compositions, having MIDI connectors built into your audio interface saves you from the need to acquire one more box.

◆ **Drivers:** Okay; they're not really amenities but necessities. Before you buy any audio interface, make sure that drivers are available for it that are compatible with the version of Mac OS X you're running.

Figure 5.6 A MIDI port. For a photo of some MIDI ports, see Figure 5.9.

Hardware for Recording Software Instruments

Recording into a Software Instrument track has simpler hardware requirements than for a Real Instrument track. Stripped down to its basics, the process needs:

◆ A MIDI controller

◆ A MIDI interface

MIDI controllers are devices that usually mimic the appearance and operation of "normal" musical instruments but output no sound, just MIDI data (see Chapter 3 for an introduction to MIDI). A controller needs another piece of equipment to produce sound—for instance, your Mac running GarageBand. You can also connect a controller to an external *sound module*, which contains circuitry for generating tones from samples or by synthesizing them. MIDI keyboards can also be combined with tone-generating hardware into a single instrument. These *MIDI synthesizers* can be used as stand-alone instruments, but are much more expensive than simple controllers.

MIDI devices and MIDI cables use a distinctive type of connector not found in Macintosh hardware (**Figure 5.6**), so another piece of equipment, the *MIDI interface*, is needed to mediate between the controller and your Mac. A MIDI cable connects the MIDI controller to the MIDI interface, which in turn is connected to your Mac via a USB (or more rarely, a FireWire) cable. It is becoming more common for MIDI controllers to include simple MIDI interfaces. This allows you to plug your MIDI keyboard directly into a USB or FireWire port on your Mac, eliminating yet another box from your desk.

MIDI controllers

Most MIDI controllers are keyboards, and in fact, those are the only controllers mentioned in GarageBand's documentation or marketing materials. MIDI controllers can take other forms, however; there are MIDI controllers in the shape of guitars, there are some that look and play just like wind instruments, and there are others that imitate drums. Even though GarageBand is silent on the subject, any controller that complies with the MIDI standard should work with GarageBand, and there are anecdotal reports from a few brave souls who have successfully used non-keyboard controllers with GarageBand.

Keyboards

I'll concentrate on MIDI keyboard instruments since they're usually easier for beginners to handle. They're also cheaper than the other varieties by a long shot. Keyboards come in a range of sizes, with a variety of bells and whistles available (**Figure 5.7**). If you're a two-handed keyboard player, you'll probably want a keyboard with 49 or 61 keys (four and five octaves, respectively). Keyboard controllers that match the piano's range of 88 keys exist, too, but they cost significantly more and take up more of that precious workspace. Beginners who just want a tool for playing simple melodies into GarageBand may be happier with a two-octave model.

No matter how many keys you decide on, be sure that the keys are full-size—that is, the width and depth of piano keys. You'll see a lot of cheap keyboards with synthesizers and speakers built in but with tiny keys. They're frustrating to play, and also they normally don't have MIDI ports, so they're of no use to GarageBand as MIDI controllers.

Figure 5.7 A five-octave (61-note) MIDI controller keyboard.

And speaking of keys, MIDI keyboard controllers can have several different types of key action, which provide varying levels of responsiveness (as well as varying levels of cost):

- **Synth action:** This is the simplest mechanism. The key is merely a switch and provides no tactile feedback.

- **Weighted action:** When you press a key, you feel some resistance, akin to the feeling of playing a piano keyboard. There are different technical means of accomplishing this; the most expensive instruments use actions identical to those in grand pianos.

Other characteristics to look for in a keyboard include:

- **Touch sensitivity:** Sometimes called velocity sensitivity; a keyboard with touch sensitivity can record the pressure with which you press the key. In MIDI terms, this is the note's *velocity*, and it translates into volume when played through a Software Instrument. This feature is fairly common in MIDI controllers nowadays.

- **Aftertouch:** Some keyboards respond to the pressure of your finger on the key after the note is initially struck or to the way you remove your finger from the key. This can affect the way the sound changes during a long note, or the end of the sound once the key is released. It's a feature not often found on inexpensive keyboards.

continues on next page

HARDWARE FOR SOFTWARE INSTRUMENTS

Keyboards often have more than just keys. Many have controls that let you add inflection to your performance. GarageBand supports MIDI data for the properties of *pitch bend*, *modulation*, and *sustain*, and you can adjust the values for these qualities in the track editor (see Chapter 9 to learn about the track editor).

◆ **Pitch bend:** Many keyboards include a wheel that allows you raise or lower the pitch by tiny amounts (**Figure 5.8**). This technique is known as *bending* the pitch, and if you bend the pitch of a note while recording a Software Instrument in GarageBand, the amount of bend is also recorded.

◆ **Modulation:** The modulation wheel colors your instrument's sound by adding varying degrees of vibrato depending on how far you roll the wheel.

◆ **Sustain:** Most keyboards have a connector that allows you to attach a sustain pedal, which acts just like the pedal of the same name on a piano. If you play a key, hold down the sustain pedal, and then release the key, the note will continue to sound as long as your foot is on the pedal.

MIDI interfaces

As mentioned earlier, a MIDI interface is a piece of equipment that allows MIDI devices to connect to computers. It can be as simple as a cable with a pair of MIDI In/Out connectors at one end and a USB connector at the other, with some electronics contained in a bulge somewhere around the middle. For GarageBand, that's probably all you need. In fact, chances are good that it's more than you need, because many newer models of MIDI keyboard incorporate MIDI interfaces, so you can connect the keyboard directly to your Mac with a USB cable (**Figure 5.9**).

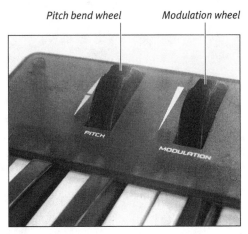

Pitch bend wheel   Modulation wheel

Figure 5.8 Pitch bend and modulation wheels on a MIDI keyboard.

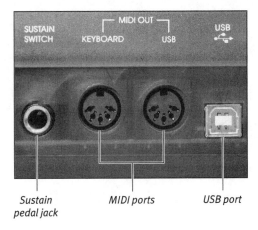

Sustain pedal jack   MIDI ports   USB port

Figure 5.9 Connectors on the back of a MIDI controller with an integrated MIDI interface, showing MIDI In and MIDI Out ports, a USB port, and a jack for connecting a sustain pedal.

If you need to connect multiple MIDI instruments to your Mac simultaneously, you can spend more money and get an interface with 2, 4, or 8 sets of MIDI In and Out ports. Some of these devices will connect to your Mac via FireWire, whose greater bandwidth can more easily handle multiple channels of data. Remember, however, that GarageBand can record only one track at a time, so the data from all of your instruments will be condensed into a single track and use the sound of one Software Instrument.

Features to look for in MIDI equipment

When choosing MIDI equipment, look for the following features. Some of these will be familiar from our discussion of audio recording equipment.

◆ **Bus power:** Devices that get their juice from the USB or FireWire bus don't need a separate power adapter.

◆ **Integration with audio:** If you can find a unit that combines a MIDI interface with an audio interface, you have one less piece of equipment to worry about.

◆ **Drivers:** Before you buy a piece of MIDI hardware, check to see that its manufacturer has updated its drivers for compatibility with the version of Mac OS X you're using.

A special note: Look for MIDI devices that say they are "USB-MIDI class compliant." That means that they use the default MIDI driver built into Mac OS X and don't need a separate driver.

Hardware for Playback

By default, when you click the Play button in GarageBand, your song plays back through the speakers built into your Mac. This is likely to prove disappointing, as these internal speakers are definitely lo-fi. You won't hear the full spectrum of tonal color produced by GarageBand's instruments, and your own performance will sound wan and anemic.

As long as you've gone to the trouble of adding a good audio interface to your setup, you should also invest in a good pair of speakers and/or headphones. Headphones are especially useful if you often record live performances. They let you monitor the recording without bothering the participants or the audience. They also let you work on your songs late at night and not disturb the neighbors.

Plug your speakers or headphones into the outputs of your audio interface (rather than directly into your Mac) so you can take advantage of the higher-quality audio circuitry. Internal audio interfaces don't always provide headphone jacks, but external interfaces do, almost without exception.

Setting Audio Preferences

After you've hooked up all this great equipment, you have to tell GarageBand to use it. For this task, use the Audio/MIDI pane of the GarageBand Preferences dialog to choose which devices to use for audio input and output. Fortunately, thanks to the native support for MIDI built into Mac OS X, GarageBand finds your MIDI devices automatically.

Preparing Hardware to Recognize GarageBand

Some audio interfaces work only with a specific set of applications. You may have to tell your audio device that it's okay to talk to GarageBand. If you think this may be the case, consult your hardware's documentation for more information.

The Digidesign Mbox is a case in point. Before it will work with GarageBand, GarageBand has to be added to its list of supported applications.

This is easy enough to do. Open the application CoreAudio Setup (it should be in the Digidesign folder along with Pro Tools LE) and click the Supported Applications button in the Digidesign CoreAudio Setup dialog (**Figure 5.10**).

In the Digidesign CoreAudio Supported Applications dialog, click Add New Application (**Figure 5.11**) and navigate to your copy of GarageBand. Select GarageBand and click the Choose button, and GarageBand will be added to the list of supported applications. Click Done two more times, and now you really are done!

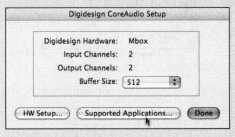

Figure 5.10 The Digidesign CoreAudio Setup dialog.

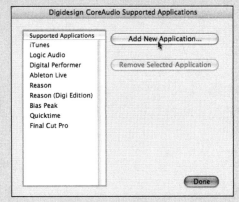

Figure 5.11 The Digidesign CoreAudio Supported Applications dialog.

To choose audio devices:

1. Choose GarageBand > Preferences (Command-,).

   The Preferences dialog opens to the General tab (**Figure 5.12**).

2. Click the Audio/MIDI button to display the Audio/MIDI tab (**Figure 5.13**).

   By default, GarageBand is set to use your computer's built-in audio hardware for input and output.

3. From the Audio Output pop-up menu, choose the device you want to use for output (**Figure 5.14**).

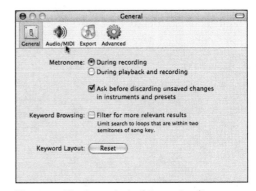

Figure 5.12 The General tab of GarageBand's Preferences dialog.

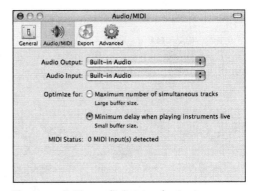

Figure 5.13 Setting audio input and output preferences for GarageBand.

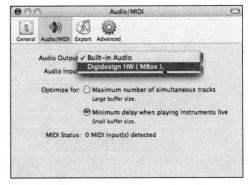

Figure 5.14 Choosing a device to use for audio output.

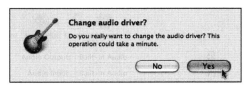

Figure 5.15 You're given a chance to change your mind before changing audio drivers.

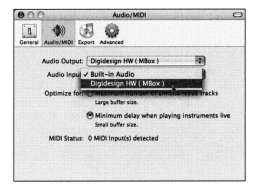

Figure 5.16 Choosing a device to use for audio input.

4. An alert appears, asking whether you really want to change audio drivers (**Figure 5.15**). Click Yes, and after a delay, the new output is ready for use.

5. From the Audio Input pop-up menu, choose the desired input device (**Figure 5.16**).

6. The Change Audio Driver? dialog appears. Click Yes, and wait while the new driver is prepared.

RECORDING REAL INSTRUMENTS

The process of recording Real Instruments in GarageBand is similar to that for Software Instruments, but different enough that I've provided a separate chapter for each procedure. There is some duplication between the chapters, but I decided it was better to make each one complete rather than use a lot of cross-references and make you flip back and forth.

Once you have your audio equipment set up and connected to your computer, you're ready to record. Recording audio is pretty simple in GarageBand: just click the Record button, and whatever comes in through your audio inputs is captured on your computer's hard disk.

Before you click that button, you should check out some GarageBand features that will help you streamline your recording session. Here's what I cover in this chapter:

◆ Using the metronome to help you keep a steady beat while recording.

◆ Listening to your track while it's being recorded.

◆ Setting the right track recording level.

◆ Recording a new region into a Real Instrument track.

◆ Using a cycle region to re-record a portion of a track.

About Recording in GarageBand

As I said, it's easy to record in GarageBand. Recording an entire song, on the other hand, takes a bit of work. By this I mean that recording in GarageBand has significant limitations. You can record into only a single track at a time, so if you want to make a multitrack recording of your band, with drums in one track and guitar in another and a vocalist in another, you have to record the tracks one at a time. This takes a lot of the fun and spontaneity out of the whole band experience.

Alternatively, you can set up a pair of microphones in front of the band (or mike each performer individually and run the mikes through a mixer) and record the band's performance into a single track. But in that case, which Real Instrument do you assign to the track? You can record into a basic track, but then you lose out on one of GarageBand's coolest features: the preset effects settings that define each Real Instrument.

GarageBand is designed with the solo musician in mind. Thanks to the fact that GarageBand handles several types of musical materials (loops, audio recording, and MIDI data), a musician working alone can have a lot of fun producing richly textured songs with GarageBand. One way to go about it is to start by laying down a percussion track constructed from loops. Next, record a bass line using a MIDI keyboard into a Software Instrument track. Finally, record a Real Instrument track while playing guitar; or record yourself singing and add piano or guitar chords later, using another Software Instrument track.

GarageBand doesn't assume that you're going to record entire tracks at once. Each time you record a take, you create a *region* within a track. A region can be any length, from a few notes to a whole song. You can record as many regions in a track as you want, and you can start recording at any point in the timeline. This gives you tremendous flexibility: you can record small pieces of a song as inspiration strikes and then arrange them into a larger composition when you're ready (you'll learn how to do that in Chapter 8).

Using the Metronome

To help you play or sing in time, GarageBand provides a metronome. While you record, it ticks away at the tempo you set for your song. The sound of the metronome itself is not recorded. You can set the metronome to play only during recording or during both recording and playback.

To give yourself a running start, you can also set the metronome to play for a full measure, or *count-in*, before you start recording.

To use the metronome:

◆ Choose Control > Metronome (Command-U). A check mark indicates that the metronome is enabled (**Figure 6.1**).

When you click the Record button, the metronome will play a sound on each beat of your song.

To turn off the metronome:

◆ Choose Control > Metronome (Command-U). The item is now unchecked.

The metronome will no longer play during recording.

To have the metronome play a count-in before recording:

◆ Choose Control > Count In. A check mark appears next to the command (**Figure 6.2**).

When you click the Record button, the metronome will play for a complete measure before recording begins.

To disable count-in:

◆ Choose Control > Count In. The item is now unchecked.

The metronome will not play before recording starts.

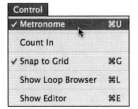

Figure 6.1 The check indicates that the metronome is on.

Figure 6.2 Setting the metronome to play a full measure before starting to record.

USING THE METRONOME

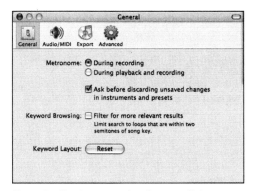

Figure 6.3 The GarageBand Preferences dialog.

To set preferences for the metronome:

1. Choose GarageBand > Preferences (Command-,) (**Figure 6.3**). The Preferences dialog opens, displaying the General pane.

2. *Choose one of the Metronome options:*

   ▲ Select During Recording to have the metronome play only while the Record button is pressed.

   ▲ Select During Playback and Recording to have the metronome play both while recording and during playback.

Monitoring

It's very helpful to practice playing or singing your part while listening to the parts of a song that are already assembled. GarageBand also lets you hear yourself, or *monitor* your track, as you play along with the rest of the song. With monitoring turned on, you can hear what your instrument or voice sounds like after filtering through your equipment and into GarageBand. The best part is that you get to hear exactly what is being recorded into the track you have selected.

You can turn monitoring on or off when you first create a track, and you can also change this setting at any time using the Track Info window.

To set monitoring for a track:

1. Select the track into which you want to record (**Figure 6.4**).

2. Open the Track Info window (Command-I) (**Figure 6.5**).

3. *Do one of the following:*
   - ▲ Click the Monitor: Off button to disable monitoring.
   - ▲ Click the Monitor: On button to turn monitoring on.

✔ Tip

- Turn off monitoring while you're not actively recording or rehearsing. If you have a microphone or an instrument connected to your computer while monitoring is on, it can pick up playback from your speakers, resulting in nasty feedback.

Figure 6.4 Selecting a track.

Figure 6.5 The Track Info window, showing the Monitor buttons.

About Setting the Recording Level

A general rule of recording is to record your signal at the highest (or "hottest") level (or volume) possible without causing distortion, or *clipping*. In GarageBand, use the level meters in each track's mixer panel to monitor its level. If the level reaches the clipping range frequently, you need to lower your recording level.

In fact, it's a very good idea to set the input level for your track before you start to record. You can test for potential clipping problems by playing or singing a few of the loudest passages from your song and watching the track level meters. Adjust your track's input so that the highest levels cause the red lights to blink briefly, but not stay lit.

Using the Track Level Meters

The track level meters indicate signal volume levels with a row of colored lights. Low signals activate only a few lights; high signals make the meter light up all the way across. When the signal hits a momentary peak, the light farthest to the right stays illuminated for an instant (**Figure 6.6**). This helps you monitor the general strength of the signal, without having to pay attention to every tiny fluctuation in the meters.

Most of the lights are green. These indicate that the signal is coming in at a safe level. The lights at the extreme right end of the meter are orange and then red, to alert you that the signal is becoming dangerously high. If the signal reaches the point of distortion, the *clipping indicator* lights up and turns red. This indicator is a separate dot just beyond the end of the meter (**Figure 6.7**). It will stay lit for the rest of the session in case your attention happened to be directed elsewhere when the clipping occurred. Lower the strength of your input signal until the clipping indicators stay dark the whole time (see the next section, "Setting Input Levels").

Once you've fixed the problem that caused the clipping indicators to come on, you should turn the indicators off again, so they can alert you to the next occurrence of clipping.

To reset the clipping indicators:

◆ Click a pair of clipping indicators that have turned red (**Figure 6.8**).
   They go dark.

Peak indicators

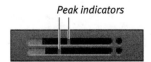

Figure 6.6 The track level meters, showing the peak indicators.

Clipping indicators

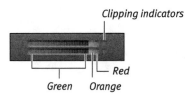

Green   Orange   Red

Figure 6.7 The track level meters during an episode of clipping. The extremely high level of the incoming signal has lit up the entire length of the meters, and the clipping indicators have been triggered.

 Figure 6.8 Resetting the clipping indicators.

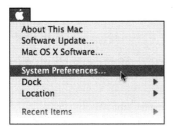

Figure 6.9 The System Preferences command on the Apple menu.

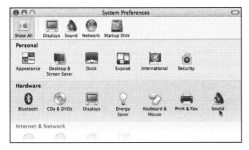

Figure 6.10 The System Preferences application opens.

Input Level indicators

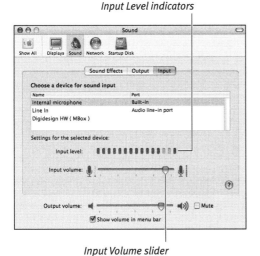

Input Volume slider

Figure 6.11 The Input tab of the Sound pane. The Input Level indicators show that the incoming signal is dangerously close to clipping.

Setting Input Levels

Use the controls on your audio interface to adjust the input level of your track. If you have an internal interface (such as a PCI card), you'll probably have to make the adjustment in software, in a control panel or dialog. If you are recording though your Mac's built in audio-in port (or a PowerBook's internal microphone), use the Sound pane in System Preferences to set your recording level.

To set the input level using System Preferences:

1. From the Apple menu, choose System Preferences (**Figure 6.9**).

   The System Preferences window opens (**Figure 6.10**).

2. Click the Sound button to open the Sound pane.

3. If the Input pane is not visible, click the Input tab (**Figure 6.11**).

4. Play or sing and watch the Input Level indicators. If you notice that the indicators frequently light up all the way across the scale, then clipping is occurring.

5. Adjust the Input Volume slider until the indicators just barely touch the right edge of the scale in the loudest passages (**Figure 6.12**).

6. Close the System Preferences window.

✔ Tip

■ If you let the mouse pointer hover over the Input Volume slider, a tool tip appears, displaying a numerical readout of the input level (**Figure 6.13**). Not terribly practical, but if you're really particular, then this might excite you.

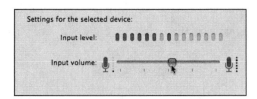

Figure 6.12 Adjusting the Input Volume slider.

Figure 6.13 The numerical value of the input level appears when you hover over the slider.

Figure 6.14 Preparing to reset the volume slider.

Figure 6.15 The volume slider at the 0 dB level.

Using the Track Mixer Volume Slider

You may be tempted to use the volume slider in the track mixer to adjust the track's level to compensate for clipping. It's far better to leave the track's volume slider at its 0 dB (zero decibel, or neutral) level, while recording, and adjust the signal level at an earlier point in the signal path, usually in the audio interface.

The track mixer volume slider is best used later in the process, at the mixing stage. At that point, when you've finished recording all your tracks, use the volume slider to adjust the balance among the individual tracks. I'll show you how to use the track volume slider in Chapter 11.

To reset the volume slider to its neutral level:

◆ In the track mixer, Option-click the volume slider (**Figure 6.14**).

It returns to the neutral (0 dB) gain position (**Figure 6.15**).

Recording into a Real Instrument Track

It's almost time to record. Here are the items on your preflight checklist:

◆ Check the amount of free space on your hard drive. Remember that recording audio at CD quality requires about 10 MB of disk space per minute of music.

◆ Check your instrument or microphone to make sure it's properly connected to your Mac and that a signal is coming through.

◆ Select a Real Instrument track to record into.

◆ Open the track's Track Info window and check that the Input channel and Format (Stereo or Mono) settings are correct. (These are the properties you set when creating the track; see "To add a Real Instrument track" in Chapter 3.) While you're there, turn on monitoring as well.

◆ Play (or sing) a few loud passages and adjust the strength of the signal using the controls on your audio interface to set the recording level for the track (see "About Setting the Recording Level" earlier in this chapter).

To record into a Real Instrument track:

1. With a Real Instrument track selected, move the playhead to the spot in the song where you want recording to begin (**Figure 6.16**).

2. Click the Record button (or press R) to start recording (**Figure 6.17**).
   The red dot in the center illuminates.

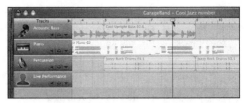

Figure 6.16 Pick a spot to begin recording.

Record button   Play button

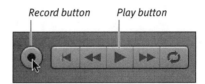

Figure 6.17 Click the Record button to start recording and the Play button to stop.

RECORDING INTO A REAL INSTRUMENT TRACK

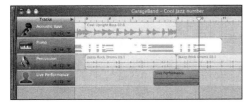

Figure 6.18 A new region appears during recording.

Figure 6.19 Your newly recorded region.

3. Begin your performance.

As you record, the playhead moves down the timeline, leaving a new region in its wake (**Figure 6.18**). You won't see anything in the new region until you stop recording and GarageBand has time to process the audio.

4. Click the Play button (or press the spacebar) to stop recording.

The playhead stops at the end of your newly recorded region (**Figure 6.19**).

5. To make additional recordings, *do one of the following:*

▲ To record another region in the same track, move the playhead to a new location and repeat steps 2 through 4.

▲ To record into another track, create a new track or select an existing track and repeat steps 1 through 4.

RECORDING INTO A REAL INSTRUMENT TRACK

117

Re-recording a Section of a Song

Suppose the first take of your recording goes swimmingly, except for one measure where you flubbed a few notes. You don't have to record the whole region over again to fix those notes—GarageBand includes a feature that lets you re-record just a portion of a region.

You do this by creating a *cycle region* that defines the passage you want to record over (**Figure 6.20**). The next time you click the Record button, only the cycle region is recorded. A new region is created in the track, splitting the original region into two parts (**Figure 6.21**).

As you record, the playhead jumps to the beginning of the cycle region and proceeds to the end and then jumps back to the start of the region and plays back the material you just recorded. The playhead continues to cycle through the region, playing the newly recorded material, until you click the Play button to stop playback. Recording is enabled only on the first pass, though. If you don't like what you just recorded, repeat the procedure.

To record over part of a song:

1. Click the Cycle button in the transport controls below the timeline (**Figure 6.22**).

   A second ruler appears below the beat ruler; a portion of it is colored yellow, indicating the cycle region. If this is the first time you've invoked the cycle region for this song, the cycle region will encompass the first four measures. If you have used the cycle region before in this song, GarageBand displays the cycle region at its previous location.

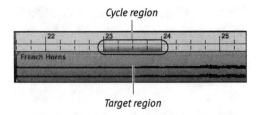

Cycle region

Target region

Figure 6.20 A one-measure cycle region defined, before recording.

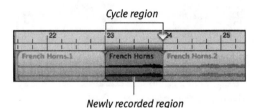

Cycle region

Newly recorded region

Figure 6.21 After recording using the cycle region. A new region has been created in the selected track.

Figure 6.22 The Cycle button.

Figure 6.23 Dragging the cycle region to a new position.

Figure 6.24 Resizing the cycle region.

2. Drag the cycle region so it covers the portion of the timeline you want to record again (**Figure 6.23**).

3. To resize the region, move the mouse pointer over either end. The pointer turns into the Resize tool (**Figure 6.24**). Drag either end of the region to resize it.

4. Select the track into which you want to record.

5. Click the Record button (or press R) to begin recording.

6. Begin playing or singing.

While you are recording, the playhead moves through the cycle region. A new region appears in the cycled portion of the timeline, containing your newly recorded material (Figure 6.21). When the playhead reaches the end of the cycle region, it jumps back to the beginning and repeats, this time playing back the new region you just recorded.

7. Click the Play button (or press the spacebar) to stop recording.

8. *Do one of the following:*
   ▲ If you want to record over the cycle region again, click Record (or press R) to start the procedure again.
   ▲ If you are satisfied with the new recording, click the Cycle button again to hide the cycle region.

✔ Tips

■ Other audio programs call this technique *punching in* and *punching out* and refer to the ends of the cycle region as *punch-in* and *punch-out points*.

■ When you're satisfied with the results of your cycle recording, you can fuse the newly recorded region with the pieces of the original region to form a single unit. (See "Joining Regions" in Chapter 8.)

Real vs. Software Instrument Cycle Regions

When you record into a Software Instrument track, the cycle region operates differently. As long as the playhead keeps repeating its path through the cycle region, GarageBand stays in Record mode. Anything you play during the same recording cycle will be added to the material recorded on the previous passes.

In other words, you can continue to record that difficult passage over and over until you get it right!

RECORDING SOFTWARE INSTRUMENTS

The process of recording Software Instruments in GarageBand is similar to that for Real Instruments, but different enough that I've provided a separate chapter for each procedure. There is some duplication between the chapters, but I decided it was better to make each one complete rather than use a lot of cross-references and make you flip back and forth.

Once your MIDI hardware is set up and connected to your computer, you're ready to record. The act of recording into a Software Instrument track is simple: click the Record button, and whatever data comes in through your MIDI interface is captured on your computer's hard disk.

Before you click that button, you should check out some GarageBand features that will streamline your recording session. Here's what I cover in this chapter:

◆ An overview of recording in GarageBand.

◆ Using GarageBand's onscreen keyboard and a suggestion for an alternative.

◆ Using the metronome to help you keep a steady beat while recording.

◆ Recording a new region into a Software Instrument track.

◆ Using a cycle region to re-record a portion of a track.

About Recording in GarageBand

As I said, it's easy to record in GarageBand. Recording an entire song, on the other hand, takes a bit of work. By this I mean that recording in GarageBand has significant limitations. You can record into only a single track at a time, so if you want to make a multitrack recording of your band, with drums in one track and guitar in another and a vocalist in another, you have to record the tracks one at a time. This takes a lot of the fun and spontaneity out of the whole band experience.

Alternatively, you can set up a pair of microphones in front of the band (or mike each performer individually and run the mikes through a mixer) and record the band's performance into a single track. But in that case, which Real Instrument do you assign to the track? You can record into a basic track, but then you lose out on one of GarageBand's coolest features: the preset effects settings that define each Real Instrument.

GarageBand is designed with the solo musician in mind. Thanks to the fact that GarageBand handles several types of musical materials (loops, audio recording, and MIDI data), a musician working alone can have a lot of fun producing richly textured songs with GarageBand. One way to go about it is to start by laying down a percussion track constructed from loops. Next, record a bass line using a MIDI keyboard into a Software Instrument track. Finally, record a Real Instrument track while playing guitar; or record yourself singing and add piano or guitar chords later, using another Software Instrument track.

GarageBand doesn't assume that you're going to record entire tracks at once. Each time you record a take, you create a *region* within a track. A region can be any length, from a few notes to a whole song. You can record as many regions in a track as you want, and you can start recording at any point in the timeline. This gives you tremendous flexibility: you can record small pieces of a song as inspiration strikes and then arrange them into a larger composition when you're ready (you'll learn how to do that in Chapter 8).

ABOUT RECORDING IN GARAGEBAND

Working with the Onscreen Music Keyboard

For those without MIDI hardware, GarageBand includes a virtual keyboard: a picture of a keyboard, which you play by clicking the keys with the mouse. The onscreen keyboard acts as a substitute for a "real" MIDI keyboard. Any notes you play on it are sent to the selected Software Instrument track. If you are recording, the notes you play are recorded, just as if you had played them on a piece of hardware.

The keyboard is rather clumsy, and it's not useful for entering lively melodies. It comes in handy, though, if you're trying to get some work done in GarageBand while you're away from your studio—traveling with a PowerBook, for example. It works well for recording long-held notes, and it's useful for trying out unfamiliar Software Instruments to see how they sound.

To display the onscreen keyboard:

◆ With a Software Instrument track selected, choose Window > Keyboard (Command-K).

The onscreen keyboard appears (**Figure 7.1**) bearing the name of the currently selected Software Instrument track.

If you select a Real Instrument track while the keyboard is displayed, the keyboard dims and becomes inactive (**Figure 7.2**).

Close button

Zoom button

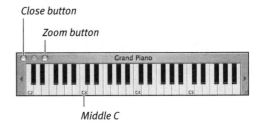

Middle C

Figure 7.1 GarageBand's onscreen keyboard. The name of the currently selected track is displayed at the top.

Figure 7.2 The keyboard is now unavailable for use.

Figure 7.3 Playing the keyboard with the mouse.

To hide the onscreen keyboard:

◆ If the keyboard is displayed, *do one of the following:*

▲ Choose Window > Keyboard (Command-K).

▲ Click the Close button in the upper-left corner of the keyboard.

The keyboard disappears.

To use the onscreen keyboard:

◆ Click a key on the keyboard (**Figure 7.3**). GarageBand sounds the note, using the selected Software Instrument track.

Playing Softly and Loudly

GarageBand's onscreen keyboard allows you to reproduce the effect of applying varying degrees of pressure to a physical key to create notes of different volume levels. And no, it doesn't depend on how vigorously you press the mouse button.

Click near the key's front edge to produce a loud tone (**Figure 7.4**). The farther toward the back of the key you click, the softer the tone produced (**Figure 7.5**).

The volume of each note is recorded as velocity data and can be edited using the track editor (see Chapter 9 for more information about using the track editor).

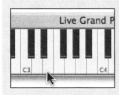

Figure 7.4 Clicking here plays a note *forte*, or loudly.

Figure 7.5 Click here to play *piano*, or softly.

Configuring the Onscreen Keyboard

For a tool of limited practicality, the onscreen keyboard itself is remarkably flexible as a user-interface element. You can resize it and change its pitch up or down to a different octave. It's even touch sensitive (see the sidebar "Playing Softly and Loudly" earlier in this chapter).

By default, the keyboard spans four octaves. In this configuration, the lowest note (labeled "C2") is equivalent to C below middle C on a piano keyboard. The keyboard can expand up to $10^1/2$ octaves—far wider than the range of any physical keyboard (concert grand pianos top out at 8 octaves). You can reduce its range to a minimum of 2 octaves.

You can access notes outside the keyboard's current display by shifting its range up or down by octaves. The lowest note of the keyboard is always a C.

To resize the keyboard:

1. Position the mouse pointer over the lower-right corner of the keyboard (**Figure 7.6**).

2. *Do one of the following:*
   - ▲ Drag to the right to widen the keyboard's range (**Figure 7.7**).
   - ▲ Drag to the left to shrink the keyboard.

✔ Tip

- To quickly expand the keyboard to its full 10-octave-plus extent, click the zoom button in the keyboard's upper-left corner (**Figure 7.8**). Clicking the zoom button again snaps the keyboard back to its previous size.

Figure 7.6 Ready to resize the keyboard.

Figure 7.7 After dragging the corner of the keyboard to the right.

Zoom button

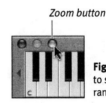

Figure 7.8 Click the zoom button to snap the keyboard to its full range.

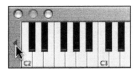

Figure 7.9 Top: Clicking the left-pointing triangle moves the keyboard's range down an octave. Notice that the lowest note of the keyboard is C2. Bottom: After you shift the range, the lowest note of the keyboard is now C1.

To change the range of the keyboard:

◆ *Do one of the following:*

▲ Click the triangle at the left end of the keyboard to shift the keyboard's range downward by an octave (**Figure 7.9**).

▲ Click the triangle at the right end of the keyboard to shift the keyboard's range upward by an octave.

MIDIKeys

Chris Reed's excellent utility MIDIKeys gives GarageBand users a keyboard substitute that is far superior to GarageBand's onscreen model (**Figure 7.10**). MIDIKeys, too, includes an onscreen keyboard, but that's not its most useful feature. It lets you use your computer's keyboard (with its keys of the good old QWERTY variety) as a MIDI keyboard.

This substitute keyboard works amazingly well. With a little practice, entering melodies is a snap. You can even play chords by holding down multiple keys at once (up to between six and eight at a time—the limit varies from keyboard to keyboard). Best of all, the program is free!

Download the software from the author's Web site:

www.manyetas.com/creed/

Figure 7.10 The MIDIKeys keyboard.

Using the MIDI Status Light

Buried among the LED-like digits of the time display is a tiny indicator that tells you whenever GarageBand receives a signal from a MIDI instrument. No bigger than a period, this little dot blinks momentarily whenever a key is pressed or released (to MIDI's way of thinking, these are separate events) (**Figure 7.11**).

The MIDI status light can be a useful troubleshooting tool. Everyone who works with MIDI will someday experience the frustrating experience of playing a note on a keyboard and getting no sound. Of course, in any complex system (including your GarageBand setup), there are myriad things that can go wrong, but the MIDI status light helps you isolate the problem. If you press the key and the MIDI status light appears, then GarageBand is getting MIDI data from your keyboard, and you know the trouble lies elsewhere. If the MIDI status light remains dark, then you know it's time to start troubleshooting your MIDI gear.

MIDI status light

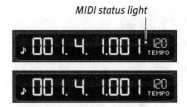

Figure 7.11 Top: The time display, showing the MIDI status light on. Bottom: No MIDI signal is being received, so the light goes out.

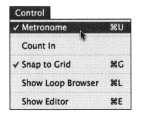

Figure 7.12 The check indicates that the metronome is on.

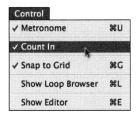

Figure 7.13 Setting the metronome to play a full measure before starting to record.

Using the Metronome

To help you play or sing in time, GarageBand provides a metronome. While you record, it ticks away at the tempo you set for your song. The sound of the metronome itself is not recorded. You can set the metronome to play only during recording or during both recording and playback.

To give yourself a running start, you can also set the metronome to play for a full measure, or *count-in*, before you start recording.

To use the metronome:

◆ Choose Control > Metronome (Command-U). A check mark indicates that the metronome is enabled (**Figure 7.12**).

 When you click the Record button, the metronome will play a sound on each beat of the song.

To turn off the metronome:

◆ Choose Control > Metronome (Command-U). The item is now unchecked.

 The metronome will no longer play during recording.

To have the metronome play a count-in before recording:

◆ Choose Control > Count In. A check mark appears next to the command (**Figure 7.13**).

 When you click the Record button, the metronome will play for a complete measure before recording begins.

To disable count-in:

◆ Choose Control > Count In. The item is now unchecked.

The metronome will not play before recording starts.

To set preferences for the metronome:

1. Choose GarageBand > Preferences (Command-,) (**Figure 7.14**).

   The Preferences dialog opens, displaying the General pane.

2. *Choose one of the Metronome options:*

   ▲ Select During Recording to have the metronome play only while the Record button is pressed.

   ▲ Select During Playback and Recording to have the metronome play both while recording and during playback.

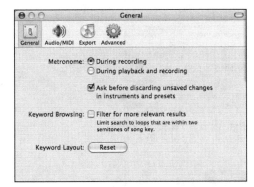

Figure 7.14 The GarageBand Preferences dialog.

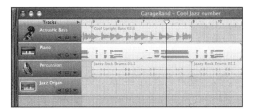

Figure 7.15 Pick a spot to begin recording.

Record button   Play button

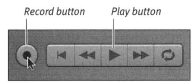

Figure 7.16 Click the Record button to start recording, and the Play button to stop.

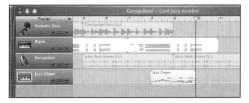

Figure 7.17 A new region appears during recording.

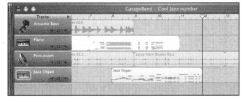

Figure 7.18 Your newly recorded region.

Recording into a Software Instrument Track

It's almost time to record. Here are the items you should have on your preflight checklist:

◆ Check your MIDI instrument and interface (if applicable) to make sure they are properly connected to your Mac and that a signal is coming through.

◆ Select a Software Instrument track to record into.

◆ Play a few notes on the instrument and make sure sound comes out of your Mac.

To record into a Software Instrument track:

1. With a Software Instrument track selected, move the playhead to the spot in the song where you want recording to begin (**Figure 7.15**).

2. Click the Record button (or press R) to start recording (**Figure 7.16**).

    The red dot in the center illuminates.

3. Begin your performance. Any notes you play on your MIDI keyboard (or enter by clicking the onscreen keyboard) will be recorded. Also, if you use the Pitch Bend or Modulation controller or the Sustain pedal, that information will be recorded, too.

    As you record, the playhead moves down the timeline, leaving a new region in its wake (**Figure 7.17**).

4. Click the Play button (or press the spacebar) to stop recording.

    The playhead stops at the end of your newly recorded region (**Figure 7.18**).

continues on next page

5. To make further recordings, *do one of the following*:

▲ To record another region in the same track, move the playhead to a new location and repeat steps 2 through 4.

▲ To record into another track, create a new track or select an existing track and repeat steps 1 through 4.

Recording Software Instrument Drums

The job of recording Software Instrument drum kits poses particular challenges. These instruments, like MIDI drum sounds in general, contain many different percussion sounds, each of which is assigned to a different note on the keyboard.

The GarageBand Help file recommends that you make a chart listing the sound or instrument played by each note on the keyboard (**Figure 7.19**), but this is a difficult (not to mention tedious) task. It's also unnecessary. GarageBand's drum kits follow the General MIDI specification pretty closely, so you can use **Table 7.1** as a guide. GarageBand's drums have more sounds than the four octaves defined in the specification, and they do deviate from the spec in places, so you'll still need to do a quick test of the full range of the Software Instrument to find all of its sounds.

The Software Instruments that model acoustic drums (like the Pop Kit and Rock Kit) follow the General MIDI list more closely than the instruments that re-create digital drum pads (like the Dance Kit and Electro Kit). The digital kits use a number of electronic sounds that don't match the General MIDI sounds. You can distinguish the two by their icons:

Acoustic drums:

Electronic drums:

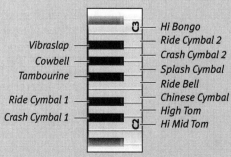

Figure 7.19 Part of a map showing the key mappings of percussion sounds.

Table 7.1

General MIDI Percussion Key Map			
KEYBOARD NOTE	INSTRUMENT	KEYBOARD NOTE	INSTRUMENT
B0	Acoustic Bass Drum	B2	Ride Cymbal 2
C1	Bass Drum	C3	Hi Bongo
C#1	Side Stick	C#3	Low Bongo
D1	Acoustic Snare	D3	Mute Hi Conga
D#1	Hand Clap	D#3	Open Hi Conga
E1	Electric Snare	E3	Low Conga
F1	Low Floor Tom	F3	High Timbale
F#1	Closed Hi Hat	F#3	Low Timbale
G1	High Floor Tom	G3	High Agogo
G#1	Pedal Hi Hat	G#3	Low Agogo
A1	Low Tom	A3	Cabasa
A#1	Open Hi Hat	A#3	Maracas
B1	Low Mid Tom	B3	Short Whistle
C2	Hi Mid Tom	C4	Long Whistle
C#2	Crash Cymbal 1	C#4	Short Guiro
D2	High Tom	D4	Long Guiro
D#2	Ride Cymbal 1	D#4	Claves
E2	Chinese Cymbal	E4	Hi Wood Block
F2	Ride Bell	F4	Low Wood Block
F#2	Tambourine	F#4	Mute Cuica
G2	Splash Cymbal	G4	Open Cuica
G#2	Cowbell	G#4	Mute Triangle
A2	Crash Cymbal 2	A4	Open Triangle
A#2	Vibraslap		

RECORDING A SOFTWARE INSTRUMENT TRACK

Re-recording a Section of a Song

Suppose the first take of your recording goes swimmingly, except for one measure where you flubbed a few notes. You don't have to record the whole track over again to fix those notes—GarageBand includes a feature that lets you re-record just a portion of a track.

You do this by creating a *cycle region* that includes the passage you want to record over again (**Figure 7.20**). The next time you click the Record button, only the cycle region is recorded. A new region is created in the track, splitting the original region into two parts (**Figure 7.21**).

When recording starts, the playhead jumps to the beginning of the cycle region and proceeds to the end and then jumps back to the start of the region. The playhead continues to cycle through the region until you click the Play button to stop. To correct a mistake, play during the first time cycling through the region; then listen to the playback on the second cycle.

GarageBand is recording the whole time, so if you play during several repetitions of the cycle, everything you play is recorded. This can sound like a train wreck if you're not careful, but it's useful for building a track by overdubbing (see the sidebar "Using a Cycle Region for Overdubbing" later in this chapter). If you click Record again after stopping, the cycle is wiped clean, and you can begin afresh.

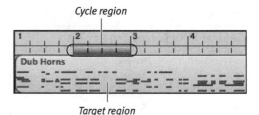

Cycle region

Target region

Figure 7.20 A one-measure cycle region defined, before recording.

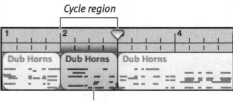

Cycle region

Newly recorded region

Figure 7.21 After recording using the cycle region. A new region has been created in the selected track.

Real vs. Software Instrument Cycle Regions

When you record into a Real Instrument track, the cycle region operates differently. GarageBand records only on the first pass through the region. The subsequent passes allow you to hear what you just recorded, but not to record anything new.

If you want to re-record over the cycle region, you have to stop recording and make a fresh start. See Chapter 6 for more information on recording Real Instrument tracks.

Figure 7.22 The Cycle button.

Figure 7.23 Dragging the cycle region to a new position.

Figure 7.24 Resizing the cycle region.

To record over part of a song:

1. Click the Cycle button in the transport controls below the timeline (**Figure 7.22**) or press C.

   A second ruler appears below the beat ruler; a portion of it is colored yellow, indicating the cycle region. If this is the first time you've invoked the cycle region for this song, the cycle region will encompass the first four measures. If you have used the cycle region before in this song, GarageBand displays it at its previous location.

2. Drag the cycle region so it covers the portion of the timeline you want to record again (**Figure 7.23**).

3. To resize the region, move the mouse pointer over either end. The pointer turns into the Resize tool (**Figure 7.24**). Drag either end of the region to resize it.

4. Select the track into which you want to record.

5. Click the Record button (or press R) to begin recording.

6. Play your instrument.

   While you are recording, the playhead moves through the cycle region. A new region appears in the timeline, containing your newly recorded material. When the playhead reaches the end of the cycle region, it jumps back to the beginning and starts through the cycle region again. This time, you can either listen to the performance you just recorded or keep playing to record fresh material on top of what you've already recorded.

continues on next page

RE-RECORDING A SECTION OF A SONG

7. Click the Play button (or press the space-bar) to stop recording.

8. If you are satisfied with the new recording, click the Cycle button again to hide the cycle region.

✔ Tips

■ Other audio programs call this technique *punching in* and *punching out* and refer to the ends of the cycle region as *punch-in* and *punch-out points.*

■ When you're satisfied with the results of your cycle recording, you can fuse the newly recorded region with the pieces of the original region to form a single unit. (See "Joining Regions" in Chapter 8.)

Using a Cycle Region for Overdubbing

Overdubbing refers to the technique of making multiple recording passes over the same part of a track. In GarageBand, it's a good way of constructing a percussion part using Software Instruments, and you can use a cycle region to accomplish it.

A live drummer plays multiple instruments at once to create a rich percussion texture. Usually, the lowest-sounding drums reinforce beats 1 and 2, with brighter sounds on beats 3 and 4. The whole texture is topped by a lively sound moving at a quicker clip, perhaps a cymbal or hi hat playing in eighth or sixteenth notes.

You can reproduce that kind of percussion sound working by yourself in GarageBand. Set up a cycle region in a Sound Instrument percussion track and play a different rhythmic pattern on a different key on each recording cycle (**Figure 7.25**). For example, on the first cycle play C1 (Bass Drum 1) on the strong beats, on the second cycle play F1 (Low Floor Tom) on the weak beats, and on the third cycle play G#1 (Pedal Hi Hat) on every eighth note.

Beware though: If you stop recording and try to overdub more notes later, you'll erase what you just recorded. Overdubbing works only during a continuous series of passes through the cycle.

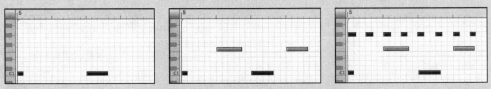

Figure 7.25 Overdubbing a percussion track, using a cycle region (shown here as seen in the track editor, for greater clarity). Top: The first pass through the cycle. Middle: The second pass. Bottom: The third pass.

Part 2: Polishing Your Song

Arranging Regions in the Timeline

8

Now that you've brought all the pieces of your song into the timeline, it's time to start polishing the composition. Maybe the guitar solo goes on too long, or the background string accompaniment needs to start earlier. What you have at this point is a rough draft; now it's time to refine it.

The first thing to do is to make sure that the general shape of the song is right. Adjusting when parts start and end, arranging sections so they come in the right order, and setting up passages to repeat are all part of the process. This is easily accomplished in GarageBand, because every item you've put into the song is a region, and regions can be arranged (moved, resized, and looped) simply by dragging them.

In this chapter, I discuss:

◆ How regions work.

◆ Selecting regions.

◆ Using the Copy, Paste, and Cut commands.

◆ Moving and resizing regions.

◆ Splitting and joining regions.

About Regions

Each morsel of music that you've placed into a track in the timeline, whether it's a four-minute continuous recording or a four-beat bass loop, is a *region* in GarageBand-speak.

A region is a copy of the original audio or MIDI recording or loop, which is stored as a file on your computer's hard disk. Any edits you make to a region do not affect the original file on which the region is based.

For example, your Apple Loops library consists of hundreds of individual audio and MIDI files. When you drag a loop from the loop browser into the timeline, GarageBand creates a copy of the loop and places it into your song. The original loop file is untouched.

The same principle (though with some differences) operates with regard to recordings you make yourself. When you make an audio recording, for example, the recording is stored as an audio file on your hard disk. If you split the region representing the recording in the timeline into two new regions, each new region can access all of the data in the original audio file.

Color Coding

GarageBand color codes the regions in the timeline so you can tell at a glance what sort of data they contain:

◆ *Purple* indicates Real Instrument regions that you recorded.

◆ *Blue* denotes Real Instrument regions that originated as loops.

◆ *Green* designates Software Instrument regions (both Apple Loops and regions you record yourself).

About Editing Regions

You do your basic editing of regions in the timeline. Regions can be moved within a track, moved to other tracks of the same type, copied and pasted, or deleted from the timeline altogether. Regions can also be resized, split, joined together, and made to repeat (or *loop*). To do more advanced editing, such as editing MIDI note or controller data or transposing regions up or down in pitch, you must use the track editor. I explain how to use the track editor in Chapter 9.

In general, GarageBand, like many other media-editing programs, employs *nondestructive editing*, which means that when you edit a region, the original disk file from which the region was derived remains unchanged. GarageBand's implementation of nondestructive editing differs significantly from that in other programs, however.

Most programs that incorporate nondestructive editing display a list of all the media available to the program. This list includes all of the recordings you have made, as well as the loops you have added to the project. The list is separate from the timeline, so even if you were to delete all regions based on a single recorded file from the timeline, that recording would still be on your media list and available for use again as a source of new regions.

In GarageBand, your recordings are represented only by the region drawn in the timeline. If all of the regions derived from a recording you made are deleted from the timeline, the original recorded file is deleted from your hard disk.

continues on next page

GarageBand behaves in other unexpected ways. If you split a Real Instrument region into two portions, for example, each portion remains linked to the original audio file. Therefore, you can later enlarge either of the portions and recover the material that was lost in the split (**Figure 8.1**). Unfortunately, this does not work with Software Instrument regions. When a Software Instrument region is split, the resulting regions no longer have access to all the data in the original file (**Figure 8.2**).

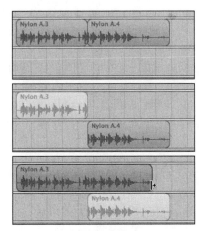

Figure 8.1 Top: A Real Instrument region is split in two. Middle: The region on the right is moved away. Bottom: The region on the left is enlarged, revealing material identical to that lost in the split.

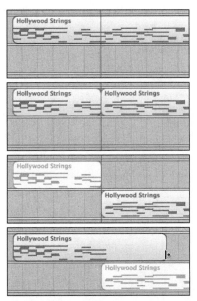

Figure 8.2 Top: A Software Instrument region before splitting. Second: The region is split. Third: The region on the right is moved away. Bottom: The region on the left is enlarged, showing that no data is left in the area split off.

Selected region

Figure 8.3 Selecting a region changes its appearance.

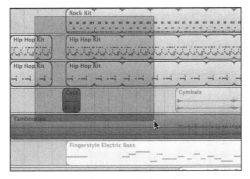

Figure 8.4 Drag-selecting multiple regions.

Figure 8.5 Selecting all of the regions in a track.

Figure 8.6 Click an area free of regions to deselect everything.

Selecting Regions

Before you perform any editing operations on a region, you must select it. You can select single regions or multiple regions, and the regions can be on different tracks. When a region is selected, its color darkens (**Figure 8.3**). You cannot select a partial region in the timeline.

To select regions:

◆ *Do any of the following:*

▲ Click anywhere within a region to select it.

▲ Click a region; then hold down the Shift key and continue to click regions you want to add to the selection. This technique is useful for regions that are scattered around the timeline.

▲ Position the mouse pointer over an empty (gray) area of the timeline and drag a selection rectangle downward and to the right over the regions you want to select (**Figure 8.4**). This technique is useful for selecting adjoining regions.

If you're still dragging when you reach the bottom of the GarageBand display and there are more tracks out of sight, the timeline will scroll upward to bring the hidden tracks into view.

▲ Click a track header to select all of the regions in the track (**Figure 8.5**).

▲ Choose Edit > Select All (Command-A) to select all of the regions in the timeline.

To deselect regions:

◆ *Do any of the following:*

▲ Shift-click any selected region to deselect it.

▲ Click anywhere in the empty (gray) area of the timeline to deselect all selected regions (**Figure 8.6**).

Basic Editing Functions

GarageBand supports the usual suite of basic editing commands: Copy, Cut, and Paste.

◆ **Copy** places a copy of the selected region into your Mac's Clipboard (a temporary storage area in memory).

◆ **Cut** also places a copy of the selected region into your Clipboard, but the original region is removed from the timeline.

◆ **Paste** places the region stored in the Clipboard into the selected track at the playhead.

You can paste into a different track, as long as it's the same type as the original track. If there is a region in the selected track at the playhead, it will be overwritten by the pasted region. You can continue to move the playhead (and/or select different tracks) and paste the same material into as many different locations as you like. You can also copy a region by Option-dragging it to a new location.

The Delete command works like the Cut command, except the regions cut from the timeline are discarded.

To copy and paste a region:

1. Select the region you want to copy (**Figure 8.7**).

2. Choose Edit > Copy (Command-C).

3. Position the playhead at the point where you want to paste the region (**Figure 8.8**).

4. Choose Edit > Paste (Command-V).
   The region is pasted into the timeline at the new position (**Figure 8.9**).

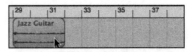

Figure 8.7 This region will be copied.

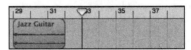

Figure 8.8 The playhead marks the spot where the region will be pasted.

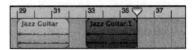

Figure 8.9 The region is pasted at the playhead.

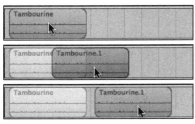

Figure 8.10 Duplicating a region by Option-dragging. Top: Hold down the Option key; then start to drag. Middle: A copy of the original region follows the mouse. Bottom: Release the mouse when the duplicate region is positioned where you want it.

To duplicate a region by dragging:

◆ Option-drag a region to a new location in the same track or in another track of the same type (**Figure 8.10**).

✔ Tip

■ Be sure to press the Option key *before* starting to drag. Otherwise, you will end up moving the region instead of duplicating it.

To cut a region:

1. Select the region you want to cut from the timeline.

2. Choose Edit > Cut (Command-X).

   The region is copied to the Clipboard and removed from the timeline. The cut region is available for pasting.

To delete a region from the timeline:

1. Select the region you want to remove.

2. Choose Edit > Delete or press Delete.

Moving Regions

You can move regions from place to place in the timeline by dragging. Regions can be moved to different locations in the same track or to other tracks of the same type. If you drag a region to a spot already occupied by another region, it overwrites the pre-existing region. As with all operations described in this chapter that involve dragging, the dragged region will snap to the timeline grid, if it is enabled (see "About the Timeline Grid" in Chapter 1).

To move a region:

◆ *Do one of the following:*

 ▲ Drag the region left or right to change its position in the track.

 ▲ Drag the region up or down to move it to a different track of the same kind.

Dragging onto Another Region

If you drag a region so it partially overlaps another region, the overlapped region shrinks to make room for the dragged region (**Figure 8.11**). The effect is the same as if you had resized the overlapped region by dragging its end toward its center (see "Resizing Regions" later in this chapter).

If you drag a region onto the middle of a larger region, the larger region is sliced in two, and both portions are reduced in size to accommodate the dragged region (**Figure 8.12**). The effect on the larger region is equivalent to using the Split command (see "Splitting Regions" later in this chapter) and then resizing the resulting fragments.

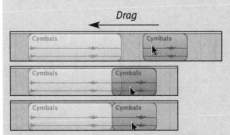 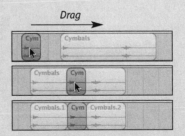

Figure 8.11 Dragging a region so it overlaps another region. Top: Drag the region on the right to the left. Middle: The regions overlap. Bottom: When you release the mouse, the right edge of the left region retreats to make room for the dragged region.

Figure 8.12 Dragging one region into the middle of another. Top: Drag the region on the left toward the middle of the region on the right. Middle: The end of the drag. Bottom: After you release the mouse, the dragged region cuts the larger region in two.

Figure 8.13 The resize pointer, positioned over the right edge of a region.

Figure 8.14 After dragging the right edge toward the left.

✔ **Tips**

■ The arrow on the resize pointer always points away from the center of the region. It doesn't tell you which way you can drag.

■ Make sure you drag the lower half of the region's boundary. If your mouse pointer strays to the upper half of the right boundary, it will turn into the loop pointer, and dragging the boundary will loop the region rather than extend it (see "Looping a Region" later in this chapter). (Nothing will happen if you drag the upper half of the left boundary of the region.)

Resizing Regions

You can shorten or lengthen a region by dragging one of its ends. Doing this changes only how much of the region is heard in your song—it doesn't change the length of the actual audio or MIDI file.

This means that if you shorten a region and then decide you've gone too far, don't despair—the material you trimmed isn't lost. Just lengthen the region again, and the previous contents of the region are restored. Compare this behavior with what happens if you split a region. Splitting a Real Instrument region results in two regions, each of which can be expanded to recover the material that was lost in the split. If you split a Software Instrument region, however, producing two regions, you cannot recover data by lengthening the regions.

If you extend a Software Instrument region beyond its original length, the extended portion will contain only silence. Real Instrument regions, on the other hand, cannot be extended beyond their original length.

To resize a region:

1. Position the mouse pointer over one of the ends of the region. Make sure the pointer is over the lower part of the region's boundary.

   The pointer turns into the resize pointer (**Figure 8.13**).

2. Drag toward the region to shorten it, or away from the region to lengthen it (**Figure 8.14**).

Looping a Region

If you want a region to repeat, you can copy it and paste it into a track several times in succession. Or you can save a few steps and loop it. Loop a region by dragging its upper-right corner to the right. Instead of lengthening the region with silence, this action appends copies of the region to itself. The upper and lower edges of the region show a notch at each repetition of the original material. The final repetition can end in mid-loop.

To loop a region:

1. Position the mouse pointer over the upper-right corner of the region you want to loop.

   The pointer becomes the loop pointer (**Figure 8.15**).

2. Drag the edge of the region to the right.

   At each repetition of the original region, a notch appears in the upper and lower edges of the region (**Figure 8.16**).

3. Release the mouse when you've created the desired number of repetitions.

✔ Tips

- If you lengthen a Software Instrument region so that silence is added to it and then loop the region, the silence is repeated along with the music in each loop.

- Once you loop a region, resizing it affects all the looped sections as well. Furthermore, you can use the Resize tool only at the edges of the original region (**Figure 8.17**).

Figure 8.15 The loop pointer includes a circular arrow.

Figure 8.16 After dragging the edge of the region with the loop pointer.

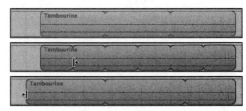

Figure 8.17 Resizing a region that has been looped. Top: The Tambourine region was made to loop twice. Middle: The pointer was placed over the right edge of the original region and dragged to the left to shorten the region. The loops were shortened as well, and more loops were automatically added to fill in the space. Bottom: Here, the left edge of the original region was dragged left, lengthening it. The other loops are similarly lengthened.

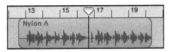

Figure 8.18 The region will be split at the playhead.

Figure 8.19 One region has become two.

Playhead

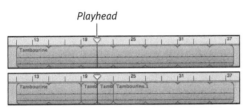

Figure 8.20 Splitting a looped region. Top: The Tambourine region has been extended by looping several times. The playhead is positioned in the middle of the second loop, where the split will occur. Bottom: After splitting, the second loop is separated from the other loops.

Splitting Regions

The Split command divides a region into two new regions at the playhead. Each resulting region can be moved, copied and pasted, or deleted just like any other region.

When you split a Real Instrument region, each of the resulting regions keeps its link with the original audio file. Either of the new regions can be extended to the full length of the original region.

To split a region:

1. Select the region you want to split.

2. Position the playhead at the spot where you want to divide the region (**Figure 8.18**).

3. Choose Edit > Split (Command-T). The region is split in two (**Figure 8.19**).

✔ Tip

■ If you split a region that's looped, GarageBand will separate the new split regions from the existing looped regions. It does this because all the repetitions in a looped region have to be the same length. Since you split one of the loops, it's no longer the same length as the others. To compensate, GarageBand takes the split repetition out of the loop, so to speak (**Figure 8.20**).

Joining Regions

Two regions of the same type can be joined together to form a new region. The two regions must be on the same track. Regions made from Real Instrument loops can't be joined, either to each other or to regions made from Real Instrument recordings.

If you are rejoining two regions that were created by splitting another region, and if you haven't altered either of them, the rejoining is very simple. It's basically equivalent to undoing the original split operation. Otherwise, when GarageBand joins two Real Instrument regions made from recordings, it creates a new audio file on disk, and the resulting joined region represents the new disk file.

To join regions:

1. Select the two regions to be joined (**Figure 8.21**).

2. Choose Edit > Join Selected (Command-J).

   ▲ If you are joining Software Instrument regions, a new Software Instrument region is created.

   ▲ If you are joining Real Instrument regions made from recordings that were not created by splitting another region, an alert dialog appears (**Figure 8.22**). Click Create to continue. A new Real Instrument region is created (**Figure 8.23**).

   The new region takes its name from the region on the left and adds the word *Merged* to the name.

✔ Tip

■ The GarageBand documentation says that to be joined, regions must be touching. This isn't exactly true. You can join regions that are separated by space (**Figure 8.24**); the space between the regions will become a silent zone in the middle of the joined region (**Figure 8.25**).

Figure 8.21 Two regions, ready for joining.

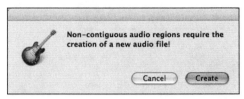

Figure 8.22 An alert warns you that merging these regions will create a new audio file.

Figure 8.23 Joining two Real Instrument regions produces a single region.

Figure 8.24 It shouldn't be possible to join these regions...

Figure 8.25 ...But it is!

ADVANCED EDITING WITH THE TRACK EDITOR

9

If you're the sort who like to likes to poke around under the hood, fiddle with custom settings, and in general, live dangerously, you'll probably end up using GarageBand's track editor at some point. It's the only window the program provides into the inner workings of the loops and recordings you've added to your song.

But if you're not that sort, don't worry. You can make plenty of great songs without ever firing up the track editor. It's completely optional. Just in case, though, I've stuffed this chapter full of information about:

- The anatomy of the track editor.

- The difference between using the track editor with Real Instrument tracks and using it with Software Instrument tracks.

- Displaying the track editor.

- Unlocking the timeline and track editor playheads.

- Renaming tracks and regions.

- Transposing regions to different keys

- Fixing the timing of notes in a Software Instrument region.

- Editing MIDI data in a Software Instrument region.

About Editing Real Instrument Regions

Unfortunately, there's not much you can do to Real Instrument regions in the track editor. You can rename them, and you can transpose regions made from Real Instrument loops but not Real Instrument recordings. There are a couple of undocumented functions, including resizing and looping, that make the track editor potentially much more useful. Because they are undocumented, alas, using them entails some risk. See the sidebar "Undocumented Features in the Track Editor" later in this chapter for more details.

ABOUT EDITING REAL INSTRUMENT REGIONS

About Editing Software Instrument Regions

The track editor is a far more powerful tool for working with Software Instrument regions than for working with Real Instrument regions. When working with a Software Instrument region, you can rename or transpose the region, adjust the timing of the notes in the region, and edit the actual notes in the region. You can also edit a number of MIDI-specific parameters that give you a lot of control over the sound of the notes.

About the Track Editor

The track editor is normally hidden, tucked out of sight at the bottom of the GarageBand window. In fact, it shares the same space as the loop browser. And like the loop browser, you can bring it out into the open with the click of a button or a simple keystroke. Its controls change depending on the type of track displayed, with more features available to Software Instrument tracks than to Real Instrument tracks. I'll describe the Software Instrument version of the track editor first and then show how the Real Instrument track editor is different (**Figure 9.1**).

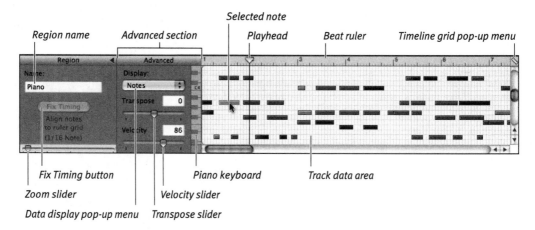

Figure 9.1 The track editor, displaying a Software Instrument region.

Some of the track editor's features will be familiar from the timeline (see "The GarageBand Interface" in Chapter 1). The *playhead* and *beat ruler* work just like their counterparts in the timeline, and the playhead's location in the beat ruler is always the same here as in the timeline. The track editor and the timeline always display the same section of a song by default. To change this setting, use the Playhead Lock button (see "Unlocking the Timeline and Track Editor Playheads" later in this chapter). The *timeline grid menu* and *zoom slider* also operate identically to the ones in the timeline, but the settings you choose here are independent of those you make in the timeline.

Most of the track editor is taken up with the *track data area*. Because the two types of tracks in GarageBand record different types of data, the track data area changes appearance drastically from one type of track to the other. Software Instrument regions are recordings of MIDI data, in which the characteristics of individual notes are recorded. Each oblong rectangle in the track data area represents a single note. Its horizontal length shows its duration, and its color shows its loudness (*velocity*, in MIDI terminology). A note's vertical position shows its pitch, using the vertical piano *keyboard* along the left edge of the track data area as a reference.

The left section of the track editor includes the *Region Name* field, which you can use to change the name of a region or track. The *Fix Timing button* is included only in the Software Instrument track editor. It lets you change the timing of notes that are off the beat by snapping them to the timeline grid. The readout below the Fix Timing button shows the timeline grid's current setting.

continues on next page

ABOUT THE TRACK EDITOR

The *Advanced section* of the track editor (which can be hidden when not needed) contains most of the editing controls. Both types of track include the *Transpose slider* for shifting the pitch of a region up or down, but the rest of the controls are unique to Software Instruments. Use the *Velocity slider* to change the loudness of a note (or of several selected notes). By default, the Software Instrument track editor shows data for notes, but you can choose to display MIDI controller data as well. Use the *Display menu* to choose the type of data to display and edit (see "Editing MIDI Controller Information" later in this chapter).

By comparison, the track editor for Real Instrument tracks is much simpler (**Figure 9.2**). Aside from the Region Name field, the only setting you can change is the Transpose slider. Because Real Instrument regions are audio recordings, the track data area uses a *waveform* graph to display the contents of the region. The track shown in Figure 9.2 was recorded in stereo, so there are two waveforms, one for each channel. A mono recording would show only one waveform. The waveform graphs the loudness (or *amplitude*) of the audio signal over time. Each bulge in the waveform represents a distinct sound event.

Region name

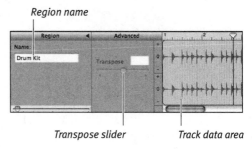

Transpose slider   Track data area

Figure 9.2 The track editor, showing a Real Instrument region.

Figure 9.3 The Track Editor button.

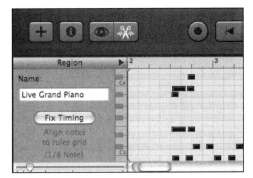

Figure 9.4 The track editor is now visible.

Figure 9.5 Double-clicking this region opens it in the track editor.

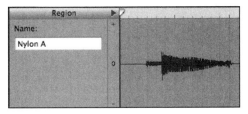

Figure 9.6 The region is ready for editing.

Displaying the Track Editor

When you first start GarageBand, the track editor is hidden, to allow more room for tracks in the timeline, but it's easy to display.

To display the track editor:

◆ If the track editor is hidden, *do one of the following:*

▲ Click the Track Editor button, near the bottom of the GarageBand window (**Figure 9.3**).

▲ Choose Control > Show Editor.

▲ Press Command-E.

The Track Editor button glows blue, and the track editor itself slides into view (**Figure 9.4**).

To hide the track editor:

◆ Click the Track Editor button or choose Control > Hide Editor (Command-E).

The track editor goes back into hiding.

To display a track in the track editor:

1. Display the track editor.

2. Click the header of the track you wish to edit.

The track appears in the track editor.

To display a specific region in the track editor:

◆ Working in the timeline, double-click the region you want to edit (**Figure 9.5**).

The track editor opens (if it is not already open) and displays the selected region (**Figure 9.6**).

✔ Tip

■ Double-clicking a region to open it in the track editor automatically unlocks the playheads (see "Unlocking the Timeline and Track Editor Playheads" later in this chapter).

Unlocking the Timeline and Track Editor Playheads

The timeline and the track editor each have their own beat ruler and playhead. The playheads are synchronized; that is, they are both located at the same spot in the song. Normally, when you play a song, the playheads move to the center of the GarageBand window, and the timeline and track editor scroll by in the background so the playheads can stay centered (**Figure 9.7**). If the two areas are at different zoom levels, they will scroll at different speeds to enable the playheads to remain in the center.

Also by default, if you drag one of the playheads, the other moves as well, so the same section of the song is always displayed in both the timeline and the track editor. You can turn off this default behavior by *unlocking* the playheads, allowing the timeline and the track editor to display different parts of the song. When you play a song with unlocked playheads, it is the playheads that move across the display; the timeline and track editor remain stationary, unless you use the scroll bars to move through the song.

To unlock the timeline and track editor playheads:

◆ Click the Playhead Lock button to unlock the playheads (**Figure 9.8**).

You can now scroll to different locations in the song in the two parts of the window.

To lock the timeline and track editor playheads:

◆ Click the Playhead Lock button to lock the playheads (**Figure 9.9**).

Both playheads will now be centered in their respective parts of the GarageBand window.

Playheads   Playhead Lock button

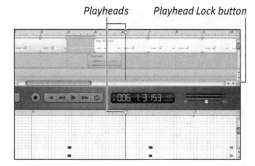

Figure 9.7 During normal playback, the playheads in the timeline and track editor both stay centered in their respective areas.

Figure 9.8 When the two triangles in the Playhead Lock button are out of alignment, the playheads are unlocked.

Figure 9.9 The playheads are locked when the triangles align.

✔ Tip

■ Using either of the horizontal scroll bars temporarily unlocks the playheads. If the playheads have been unlocked in this manner, starting playback locks them together again.

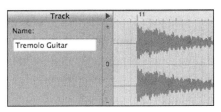

Figure 9.10 This track is ready to be renamed.

Figure 9.11 Click the empty area of the track to force the track to be selected, rather than a region in the track.

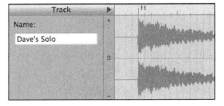

Figure 9.12 The track has a new, unique name.

Figure 9.13 The track header, showing the new name.

✔ Tip

■ The fact that clicking a track's header in the timeline causes the header in the track editor to say "Region" seems to be a bug in GarageBand 1. This behavior may change in future versions.

Renaming Tracks and Regions

When you add a track to your song, it takes its name from the instrument you assign to it in the Track Info window. If your song includes several tracks that use the same instrument, you may want to give them all unique names.

Likewise, when you record a new region, it automatically takes its name from its track. Regions created from loops are named after the loops from which they were made. Again, if your song has several regions with the same name, giving them distinctive names will help you tell them apart.

Use the track editor to rename both regions and tracks.

To rename a track:

1. If the track editor isn't open, open it now.

2. Click the track's header to select it.

   The track appears in the track editor (**Figure 9.10**).

3. Check the header at the top left of the track editor to make sure it says "Track," not "Region." If it doesn't say "Track," click somewhere in the empty gray area of the track (**Figure 9.11**).

4. In the Name field in the left quadrant of the track editor, type a new name for the track (**Figure 9.12**).

5. Press Tab or Return to confirm the new name.

   The name change is reflected in the track header (**Figure 9.13**).

To rename a region:

1. If the track editor isn't open, open it now.

2. Click the region you want to rename to select it.

   The region appears in the track editor (**Figure 9.14**).

3. Check the header at the top left of the track editor to make sure it says "Region," not "Track." If it doesn't say "Region," try clicking the region in the timeline one more time.

4. In the Name field in the left quadrant of the track editor, type a new name for the region (**Figure 9.15**).

5. Press Tab or Return to confirm the new name.

   The name change is reflected in the timeline (**Figure 9.16**).

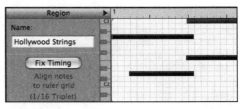

Figure 9.14 The selected region, ready for a new name.

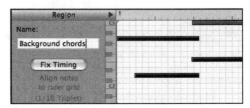

Figure 9.15 Name the region whatever you want.

Figure 9.16 The newly renamed region.

RENAMING TRACKS AND REGIONS

Expanding the Track Editor

When it first opens, the track editor provides a relatively narrow view of the data contained in a region. It can easily be expanded to display more detail.

Here's how to widen the track editor:

1. Move the mouse pointer to the area that divides the timeline from the track editor. Stay to the left of the Record button or to the right of the time display. The pointer changes into a hand (**Figure 9.17**).

2. Drag upward to widen the track editor (**Figure 9.18**). Its maximum width is almost double its default width.

Widening the track editor when a Software Instrument region is displayed increases the range of the notes spanned by the editor from 15 semitones to 27. If a Real Instrument region is displayed, widening the track editor stretches the region's waveform vertically, increasing the detail visible in the waveform.

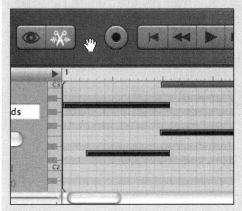

Figure 9.17 Use this hand-shaped pointer to drag the top of the track editor upward.

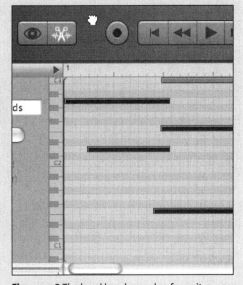

Figure 9.18 The hand has dragged as far as it can go.

About Transposition

One of the few track editor functions that works on both Real Instrument and Software Instrument regions is transposition. To transpose a region is to move it up or down in pitch, so it sounds in a different key. The unit of transposition is the *semitone*, or half-step. This is the distance between two adjacent notes on a piano keyboard: from C to C#, for example, or from E to F. Twelve semitones is equivalent to an octave, or the distance between two notes of the same name, such as C2 and C3 (**Figure 9.19**).

You can transpose both Software and Real Instrument regions, though Real Instrument regions can be transposed only if they were made from loops. This is because Real Instrument regions made from recordings don't include the extra information (the *metadata*) that tells GarageBand what key they are in to start with. Apple Loops do include this information, which allows regions made from them to be transposed.

Use transposition sparingly. Keep in mind the relationship between the key of the region you are transposing and the key of the song as a whole. Sometimes you can create a striking effect by shifting a section of a song to a different key from the main song; but you have to be sure that you transpose all the regions that are sounding together, or you'll have cacophony. Another way to use transposition is to fix mistakes, such as to correct a MIDI region that was originally recorded in the wrong key.

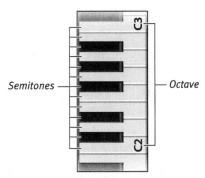

Figure 9.19 An octave spans 12 semitones.

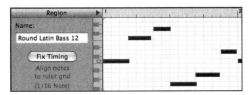

Figure 9.20 The Round Latin Bass 12 region is open in the track editor.

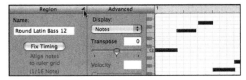

Figure 9.21 Opening the Advanced section of the track editor.

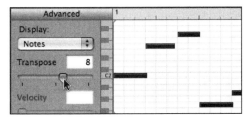

Figure 9.22 The region has been transposed up by a distance of eight semitones.

✔ Tips

- Option-click the Transpose slider to reset its value to 0.

- There is one "feature" of Software Instrument region transposition that has aggrieved a number of GarageBand users: when a Software Instrument region is transposed, the pitches displayed in the track editor do not change. The only way to tell that the region has been transposed is to look at the Transpose slider.

Transposing Software Instrument Regions

The process of transposing a Software Instrument region is fairly straightforward: move its Transpose slider left or right to shift the pitch down or up. Because the sound of a Software Instrument is artificially generated to begin with, the instrumental color of a Software Instrument region changes less drastically than does that of a Real Instrument region (see "Transposing Real Instrument Regions" later in this chapter). That's part of the reason that Software Instrument regions can be transposed up to three octaves, while Real Instrument regions have a limit of one octave.

To transpose a Software Instrument region:

1. Display a Software Instrument region in the track editor (**Figure 9.20**).

2. If the Advanced section of the track editor is not visible, click the triangle at the right edge of the track editor header to open it (**Figure 9.21**).

3. Working in the Advanced section of the track editor, *do one of the following*:
   - ▲ Drag the Transpose slider to the right to transpose the region up (**Figure 9.22**).
   - ▲ Drag the Transpose slider to the left to transpose the region down.

The maximum transposition for Software Instrument regions is 36 semitones (equivalent to three octaves) in either direction.

Transposing Real Instrument Regions

You may not be happy with the results if you transpose a Real Instrument region more than a few semitones from its original key. Digitally transposing an audio recording produces only an approximation of the sound that you would get by playing the same passage higher or lower on a physical instrument. This leads to two possible problems:

◆ Transposing a region alters the color of the sound as well as the pitch. If you transpose an acoustic guitar region down by, say, six semitones, it will likely no longer sound like a guitar.

◆ The more semitones you transpose a region from its original key, the more artificial the sound becomes. The process of digital transposition introduces errors into the data, which can sound like noise.

To transpose a Real Instrument region:

1. Display a region (it must be one that originated as a loop) in the track editor (**Figure 9.23**).

2. If the Advanced section of the track editor is not visible, click the triangle at the right edge of the track editor header to open it (**Figure 9.24**).

3. Working in the Advanced section of the track editor, *do one of the following:*

   ▲ Drag the Transpose slider to the left to transpose the region down (**Figure 9.25**).

   ▲ Drag the Transpose slider to the right to transpose the region up.

   The maximum transposition for Real Instrument regions is 12 semitones (equivalent to one octave) in either direction.

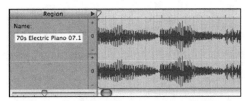

Figure 9.23 A Real Instrument loop open in the track editor, ready to be transposed.

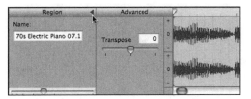

Figure 9.24 Opening the Advanced section of the track editor.

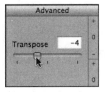

Figure 9.25 The region is transposed down 4 semitones.

✔ Tip

■ Option-click the Transpose slider to reset its value to 0.

Figure 9.26 The grid is set to ⅛ Swing Light.

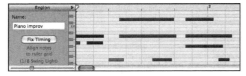

Figure 9.27 Before fixing the timing, notice that the notes don't always align with the gridlines.

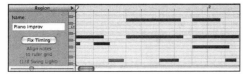

Figure 9.28 The notes have all shifted to the nearest gridlines.

✔ Tips

■ After clicking the Fix Timing button, listen to the track to see if it sounds the way you want. If you're not satisfied, use the Undo command to restore the region's previous timing. Choose a different setting from the timeline grid menu, click Fix Timing, and audition the region again.

■ The "swing" settings will give the region a jazzy feel, while the fractional note values (¼ note, ⅛ note, and so on) will impose a more rigid, "straight" feel. Be careful about fixing the timing of an entire region—you can very easily take all the life out of a performance this way. It's often better to fix individual notes that are way off and leave a few of the more subtle timing inconsistencies that make a performance sound more real.

Fixing Software Instrument Region Rhythm

One cool function of the track editor is the ability to alter the rhythmic character of an entire Software Instrument region. You can accomplish this by clicking the Fix Timing button (at the left end of the track editor), which snaps all the notes in the region to the timeline grid. If the performance that the region records was fairly stodgy, you can choose one of the Swing options from the timeline grid menu in the track editor and click the Fix Timing button to inject some life into the region.

The Fix Timing button is also handy for shaping up a region recorded by a performer who had trouble sticking with the beat. Choose a timeline grid setting of ¼ note and use the Fix Timing button to straighten out the rhythmic framework of the recording.

Note that the Fix Timing button shifts notes to the timeline grid whether or not the Snap to Grid command is checked in the Control menu.

To fix the timing of notes in a region:

1. Working in the track editor, display the Software Instrument region whose timing you want to change.

2. From the timeline grid menu in the track editor (*not* the one in the timeline), choose the grid setting you want to apply to the region (**Figure 9.26**).

   The chosen setting will be displayed in the left quadrant of the track editor (**Figure 9.27**).

3. Click the Fix Timing button.

   The notes in the region snap to the nearest gridlines (**Figure 9.28**).

Editing MIDI Data

As explained in Chapters 3 and 5, when you record a Software Instrument region, GarageBand captures data about each individual note played on a MIDI keyboard (or other MIDI controller). The track editor displays this data in graphical form and allows you to tweak these properties of any note:

◆ Length

◆ Pitch

◆ Location in time

◆ Velocity (loudness)

You can also add or delete notes and cut, copy, and paste notes using normal edit commands. You can edit several notes at once by selecting them first.

To edit individual notes:

◆ In the track editor, display the Software Instrument region you want to edit; then *do any of the following:*

▲ Click a note to select it. Shift-click or drag to select multiple notes (**Figure 9.29**). Notes turn green when selected.

▲ Drag a note up or down to raise or lower its pitch (**Figure 9.30**).

▲ Drag a note left or right to change the start of the note (**Figure 9.31**).

▲ Drag the upper-right corner of a note to the left or right to shorten or lengthen the note (**Figure 9.32**).

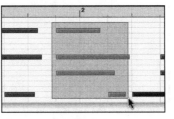

Figure 9.29 Dragging a selection rectangle around several notes.

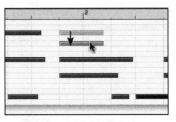

Figure 9.30 This note was dragged downward to lower its pitch by two semitones.

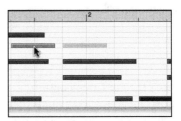

Figure 9.31 This note was dragged left so it will begin two beats earlier.

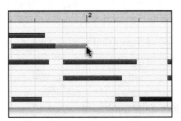

Figure 9.32 The length of this note was almost doubled by dragging.

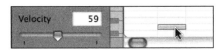

Figure 9.33 The note under the mouse pointer is selected and its original velocity is shown.

Figure 9.34 The note has turned a light gray, a visual cue that its velocity value is low.

Figure 9.35 The note has darkened, to show that it will now sound as a loud note.

Changing Note Velocity

Velocity is the MIDI term for the loudness or softness of a note. It is a measure of the force with which a key is struck. A note's velocity is indicated in the track editor by its color: the darker the note, the higher its velocity. The range of possible velocity values runs from 1 to 127.

To change a note's velocity:

1. In the track editor, display the region that contains the note whose velocity you want to change.

2. If the Advanced section of the track editor is not visible, click the triangle at the right edge of the track editor header to open it.

3. Select the note or notes whose velocity you want to edit (**Figure 9.33**); then *do one of the following:*

   ▲ Drag the Velocity slider to the left to make the note quieter (**Figure 9.34**).

   ▲ Drag the Velocity slider to the right to make the note louder (**Figure 9.35**).

   The note's color changes to reflect its new velocity value.

✔ Tips

■ An alternative method for changing the velocity of a note is to type a new value in the numerical field above the Velocity slider and then press Tab or Return.

■ If you move the Velocity slider while multiple notes are selected, each note's velocity value will be raised or lowered by the same amount. The numerical readout above the slider will show the value only for the leftmost selected note.

Adding and Deleting Notes

Ever wish you could go back and erase the flubbed notes from your last piano performance? If you had been playing a MIDI keyboard connected to a Mac running GarageBand, you could do just that. You can delete notes from a Software Instrument region in the track editor, and you can add notes as well.

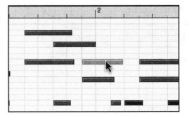

Figure 9.36 The selected note will be removed from the region.

To delete notes from a region:

1. In the track editor, display the region that you want to edit.

2. Select any note (or notes) you want to remove from the region (**Figure 9.36**).

3. Choose Edit > Delete or press Delete. The selected note is deleted (**Figure 9.37**).

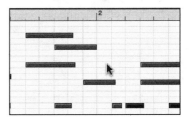

Figure 9.37 The note is gone.

To add notes to a region:

1. In the track editor, display the region you want to edit.

2. Hold down the Command key. The mouse pointer turns into a pencil (**Figure 9.38**).

3. Click the spot where you want to add a note.

   A short note of medium velocity (63) is added to the region (**Figure 9.39**).

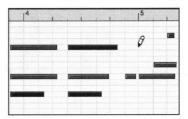

Figure 9.38 Click anywhere with the Pencil tool to add a note to the region.

✔ Tip

■ After you add a new note to the region, you can adjust its length and velocity to taste.

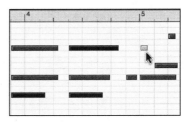

Figure 9.39 A new note appears.

Figure 9.40 Select the notes in two bars of this bass part.

Figure 9.41 The playhead is positioned two measures after the measures previously copied.

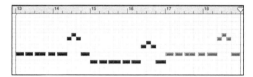

Figure 9.42 The first part of the bass line now repeats.

Using Cut, Copy, and Paste

You can also add, remove, and move notes with those old standbys: the Cut, Copy, and Paste commands. Recall that the Cut and Copy commands place selected notes on the Clipboard, a temporary storage area in your computer's memory. Cut also deletes the notes from their current location in the region. The Paste command places copies of cut or copied notes at the playhead's location.

You can paste the notes into any Software Instrument track. If the playhead is in a pre-existing region, the pasted notes will be added to that region. If the playhead is in a blank area of a track, a new region (called "Sequence") will appear in the track. It will be the same length as the region from which you copied the notes, but it will be empty except for the pasted notes.

To cut or copy notes from a region:

1. In the track editor, display the region whose notes you want to copy.

2. Select the note (or notes) to be copied (**Figure 9.40**).

3. *Do one of the following:*
   ▲ Choose Edit > Cut (Command-X). The notes are removed from the region and placed on the Clipboard.
   ▲ Choose Edit > Copy (Command-C). The notes are copied to the Clipboard.

To paste notes:

1. Following the procedure outlined in the previous task, use the Cut or Copy command to place notes on the Clipboard.

2. Position the playhead at the spot where you want to paste the notes (**Figure 9.41**).

3. Choose Edit > Paste or press Command-V. The notes are added to the track at the playhead (**Figure 9.42**).

Editing MIDI Controller Information

As explained in Chapter 5, many MIDI keyboards include controllers for performance elements such as pitch bend, modulation, and sustain. GarageBand records any input from these controllers during a performance, and you can use the track editor to edit this data. You can even enter controller data into the track editor, in case your keyboard lacks these hardware amenities.

A pop-up menu in the Advanced section of the track editor provides access to the various sets of controller data (**Figure 9.43**). The control points themselves are represented as dots connected by lines; each control point records a change in the physical state of the controller. Editing these control points is much like editing MIDI note data; you can move, cut, copy, paste, and delete the control points, and you can add new control points in the region, causing the lines that connect the control points to be redrawn in new shapes. The process of editing control points is the same for all types of controller data. Copying and pasting is most useful for transferring controller data from one region to a similar region in the same song.

To display MIDI controller data for a region:

1. Display in the track editor the region whose MIDI controller data you want to edit.

2. Click the triangle in the track editor's header to display the Advanced section of the editor, if is not already visible.

3. From the Display pop-up menu, choose the type of controller data you want to edit (Figure 9.43).

    The MIDI controller data in this region is now available for editing.

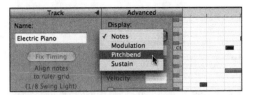

Figure 9.43 The Display pop-up menu, showing the types of MIDI controller data that can be edited in GarageBand.

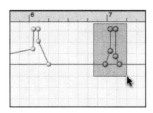

Figure 9.44 Drag-selecting a group of control points.

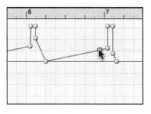

Figure 9.45 This control point was dragged upward.

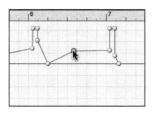

Figure 9.46 This control point was dragged to the left.

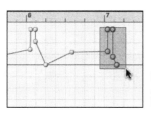

Figure 9.47 A group of points is selected.

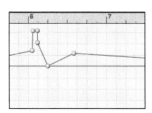

Figure 9.48 The selected points are deleted.

To edit controller information:

◆ Display the MIDI controller data for a region; then *do any of the following:*

  ▲ Click a control point to select it. Shift-click or drag to select multiple points (**Figure 9.44**). Control points enlarge slightly when selected.

  ▲ Drag a control point up or down to alter its value (**Figure 9.45**).

  ▲ Drag a control point left or right to change its position in time (**Figure 9.46**).

To delete control points:

1. In the track editor, display the region whose control points you want to edit.

2. Select any point (or points) you want to remove from the region (**Figure 9.47**).

3. Choose Edit > Delete or press Delete.

   The selected control point is deleted (**Figure 9.48**).

EDITING MIDI CONTROLLER INFORMATION

To add control points to a region:

1. In the track editor, display the region whose control points you want to edit.

2. Hold down the Command key.

   The mouse pointer turns into a pencil (**Figure 9.49**).

3. Click the spot where you want to add a control point. (**Figure 9.50**).

   A line connects it to the other control points in the region.

To cut or copy control points from a region:

1. In the track editor, display the region whose control points you want to copy.

2. Select the control point (or points) to be copied (**Figure 9.51**).

3. *Do one of the following:*

   ▲ Choose Edit > Cut (Command-X). The control points are removed from the region and placed on the Clipboard.

   ▲ Choose Edit > Copy (Command-C). The control points are copied to the Clipboard.

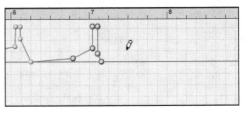

Figure 9.49 Use the Pencil tool to add control points to the region.

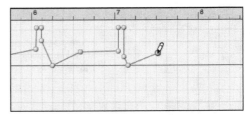

Figure 9.50 After adding several control points.

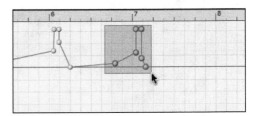

Figure 9.51 These control points will be copied.

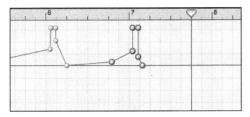

Figure 9.52 The playhead is at the spot where the copied control points will be pasted.

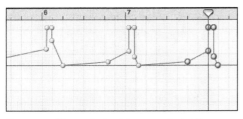

Figure 9.53 The control points are pasted at the playhead.

To paste control points:

1. Following the procedure outlined in the previous task, use the Cut or Copy command to place control points on the Clipboard.

2. Position the playhead at the spot where you want to paste the control points (**Figure 9.52**).

3. Choose Edit > Paste or press Command-V. The control points are added to the region at the playhead (**Figure 9.53**).

✔ Tips

- The track editor is a handy tool for editing MIDI controller information that you've already programmed into a track, but using it to enter a lot of data by hand is a slow and cumbersome process. There's an easier way to do it, if your MIDI keyboard is equipped with controllers for pitch bend, modulation, and sustain: add the controller data by overdubbing (see the sidebar in Chapter 7, "Using a Cycle Region for Overdubbing").

- Set up a cycle region that covers the passage to which you want to add controller data; then start recording. While the passage plays, don't touch the keys on the keyboard, but use the keyboard's hardware controllers to create the effect you want. Use a different controller on each pass through the cycle: manipulate the modulation wheel on one pass, twiddle the pitch bend wheel on another, and pump the sustain pedal on yet another. It's much more intuitive than clicking and dragging with the mouse!

EDITING MIDI CONTROLLER INFORMATION

The Types of MIDI Controller Data

GarageBand is aware of the classes of MIDI controller data that correspond to the physical controllers most commonly integrated into MIDI keyboards: pitch bend, modulation, and sustain data. Pitch bend and modulation are normally adjusted by wheel controls and are capable of recording smoothly varying data points. Sustain, on the other hand, is normally controlled by a simple on-off switch, operated by a pedal; thus, its data points always have the value 0 (for off) or 1 (for on) (**Figure 9.54**).

Values for pitch bend and modulation are graphed differently, as you can see by the different scales at the left end of the track editor when the different data types are displayed.

The pitch bend scale places 0 at the center and measures positive values above and negative values below that point (**Figure 9.55**). The scale (which runs from –60 to +60) is calibrated in arbitrary units. A pitch bend of 30 units on this scale corresponds approximately to a semitone. If a control point has a pitch bend value of +15, therefore, the pitch has been shifted upward about halfway to the next note (for example, halfway from F to F#).

The modulation scale is also calibrated in different arbitrary units, and it starts with 0 at the bottom and rises to 120 (**Figure 9.56**). The modulation controller adds vibrato to a note, and the value of a control point represents the depth of the vibrato at that point. To my ear (that's all I have to go on, because Apple has provided no documentation for this feature), a modulation setting of 120 (the maximum) creates a vibrato that fluctuates about one half semitone above and one half semitone below the pitch of the note.

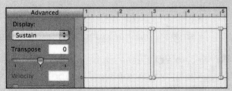

Figure 9.54 Sustain data, showing the on/off nature of the control points as they reproduce the holding down of the sustain pedal with a release every two measures.

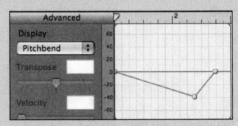

Figure 9.55 A sample of pitch bend data, showing the scale at the left end of the graph.

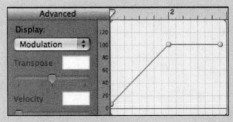

Figure 9.56 A sample of modulation data, showing the scale at the left end of the graph.

Undocumented Features in the Track Editor

GarageBand's track editor (at least in version 1.0.1 of the program) feels in many respects like a work in progress. For example, the resize and loop tools work on Real Instrument regions just like their counterparts in the timeline do (see "To resize a region" and "To loop a region" in Chapter 8). The track editor also has a tool not found in the timeline (**Figure 9.57**): a pointer that appears when you move the mouse near the upper edge of a region. When this pointer is visible, you can move the region left or right in the track editor by dragging.

Yet Apple's Help file is silent about these features. Perhaps these editing functions were insufficiently tested to warrant official presentation to the world.

The track editor harbors another undocumented feature that is definitely not ready for prime time. Through experimentation, I discovered that, working in the track editor, it's possible to use the Copy, Cut, and Paste commands on just a portion of a region, rather than an entire region. This is exactly the sort of feature that one expects of a track editor: the ability to fine-tune a recording by zeroing in on small portions of a track and trimming them away or slicing them off and moving them elsewhere.

Here's how it works: Move the mouse pointer over a Real Instrument region in the track editor. The pointer turns into a cross. Drag left or right over the passage you want to copy (**Figure 9.58**). The copied part of the region turns dark blue. Cut or copy the selected material; then position the playhead where you want to paste the material and execute the Paste command (**Figure 9.59**).

However, I've found this feature to be extremely unreliable. Sometimes the copied data isn't pasted where I expected, sometimes the track gets fouled up and won't play properly any more, and occasionally using this function crashes GarageBand and corrupts my song file.

We can only hope that Apple will polish this feature and incorporate it into an updated version of GarageBand. In the meantime, all the usual disclaimers apply: Try this at your own risk; your mileage may vary; objects may be closer than they appear.

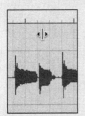

Figure 9.57 The undocumented move pointer.

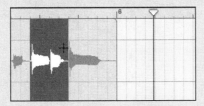

Figure 9.58 Drag with the cross pointed across the data to be cut or copied. The playhead is already positioned where we want to paste the material.

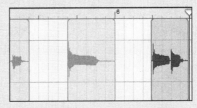

Figure 9.59 A snippet of sound has been cut from its original position and pasted several beats away.

APPLYING
EFFECTS

One feature that sets GarageBand apart from other inexpensive music programs is its collection of effects. The program includes a couple dozen of these professional-quality audio processing components. A few years ago, effects like these were found only in expensive, high-end audio programs; indeed, GarageBand's effects appear to be derived from those in Apple's flagship music program, Logic Pro.

Adding effects to your song is not a necessary part of composition, but it can make your song sound more professional and add interest. Plus, they're fun to play with. In this chapter, I discuss:

- What effects are.

- How to apply effects to individual tracks and to the song as a whole.

- How to customize effects and save the settings as presets.

- What specific effects do to the sound of your song.

- How to edit Software Instrument sounds.

- What Audio Units are and how to use them.

About Effects

Effects manipulate the sound of a track or a song electronically to enhance its sound or change the sound's color. For example, one of the most common effects is *reverb* (short for *reverberation*), which electronically alters the acoustical environment of the sound. A performance might be recorded in an acoustically dry setting, for example, like a recording studio, but with the application of reverb, the recording can sound like it was made in a large church or a tiled bathroom.

Until a few years ago, effects (which require a great deal of audio signal processing) were produced exclusively by specialized pieces of hardware. For instance, a recording studio or a sound system might have a piece of equipment devoted to adding reverb to a signal, another device might provide equalization, and still other devices might compress the dynamic range or add specialized color effects like tremolo or flanging. Acquiring all of these boxes cost serious money, and carting them around and storing them was a huge inconvenience.

Today's personal computers are powerful enough to emulate the functions of these hardware effects generators in software alone, which means that a Mac running GarageBand can take the place of quite a few of those old boxes.

In GarageBand, you use the Track Info window to apply effects to each track. I described the Track Info window for Real Instrument and Software Instrument tracks in Chapter 3 (see "About the Track Info Window"). To add effects to the entire song, you use a third type of track: the master track.

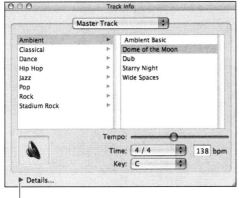

Details pane disclosure triangle

Figure 10.1 Displaying Track Info for the master track. Top: Choose Master Track from the pop-up menu. Bottom: The window now displays info for the master track.

About the Master Track

The master track is different from the tracks into which you record or into which you place loops. Unlike Real and Software Instrument tracks, it does not contain music, but it is the repository for a number of settings that affect your song as a whole. You use the master track's Track Info window to apply effects to the entire song. You can also use the master track to add volume changes over the course of a song by displaying and adjusting its track volume curve (see "Working with the Master Track Volume Curve" in Chapter 11).

To display the Track Info window for the master track:

1. Display the Track Info window for any track.

2. Choose Master Track from the pop-up menu at the top of the window.

The Track Info window displays information for the master track (**Figure 10.1**).

The Track Info Window Effects Controls

The effects controls reside in a part of the Track Info window that is hidden by default. Click the Details disclosure triangle at the bottom of the window (Figure 10.1) to reveal the effects controls (**Figure 10.2**).

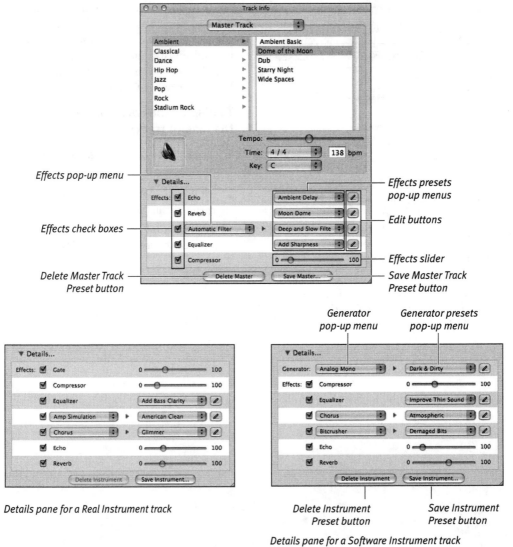

Figure 10.2 Top: The Track Info window for the master track, with effects controls now revealed. Bottom left: The Details pane for a Real Instrument track. Bottom right: The Details pane for a Software Instrument track.

You can apply effects to each track individually or to the song as a whole. To add effects to the entire song, apply them to the *master track* (see "About the Master Track" earlier in this chapter). Real Instrument and Software Instrument tracks access the same set of effects, with a few significant exceptions; a subset of these effects is available to the master track.

There are four basic effects available to all tracks: echo, reverb, equalizer (EQ), and compressor. Echo and reverb must be turned on and configured in the master track before they can be applied to any of the instrument tracks. A fifth effect, gate (short for *noise gate*), can be used only with Real Instrument tracks. The Track Info window also has a pair of pop-up menus that offer a long list of optional effects (the master track has only one menu) that may be added to the track.

The Software Instrument Track Info window includes an item that stands apart from the other effects settings. The Generator pop-up menu (together with its attendant presets menu) allows you to alter the track's basic instrumental sound. You can even replace the sound with an entirely different one. Because this procedure is somewhat different from that for adding effects, I discuss it in a separate section at the end of the chapter.

THE TRACK INFO WINDOW EFFECTS CONTROLS

Applying Effects

Applying effects to a track is not simply a matter of flicking a switch. Each effect has parameters that need to be adjusted. GarageBand takes some of the guesswork out of choosing effects settings by providing *presets* for most effects. The presets for each effect appear in a pop-up menu to the right of the effect's listing in the Track Info window. Next to each effect's presets menu is an Edit button, which opens the settings window for that effect so you can customize the effect. You can save your customized setting as a preset, and it will appear on the preset menu. Some of the simpler effects (gate and compressor, for example) are adjusted with a slider. Effects controlled with a slider do not use presets.

While you're just learning to use GarageBand, it's a good idea to stick with the presets. After you're more experienced and you've developed a more sensitive ear, then it's time to dig in and start customizing effects settings to your taste.

To apply effects to a track:

1. Open the Track Info window for the track to which you want to add effects.

2. Click the Details button to open the effects pane of the window and *do one of the following:*
   ▲ Check the box next to the name of the effect you want to add (**Figure 10.3**).
   ▲ Choose an optional effect from one of the Effects pop-up menus (**Figure 10.4**).

Figure 10.3 The check box shows that this effect is enabled.

Figure 10.4 This pop-up menu is home to some of the more exotic effects offered by GarageBand.

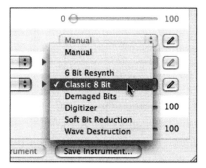

Figure 10.5 Some effects are controlled by a simple slider.

Figure 10.6 GarageBand's presets often have colorful names.

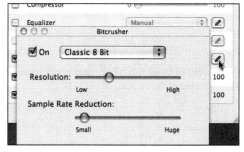

Figure 10.7 Clicking the Edit button for an effect opens a window like this.

3. Adjust the settings for the effect *using one of the following methods:*

▲ Drag the slider to choose a value for the effect (**Figure 10.5**).

▲ Choose a preset value from the effect's presets pop-up menu (**Figure 10.6**).

▲ Click the Edit button to open the settings window for the effect and drag the sliders to modify the current preset (**Figure 10.7**).

✔ Tips

■ If you customize one of the presets, the presets menu will display *Manual* until you save your changes as a new preset (see the next section, "Saving Effects Presets").

■ You can also use the settings window to turn an effect on and off or choose a preset.

Saving Effects Presets

You can save effect settings that you want to keep for later use by saving them as presets. Any presets you save will be available in all of your GarageBand songs, not just the one in which you created the preset.

To save a preset for an effect:

1. Click the Edit button for a preset to open its settings window.

2. Adjust the sliders until the effect is configured the way you want it (**Figure 10.8**).

3. From the presets pop-up menu in the settings window, choose Make Preset (**Figure 10.9**).

4. In the Make Preset dialog that appears, type the name you want to give the new preset (**Figure 10.10**).

5. Click OK.

   The new preset is added to the presets menu (**Figure 10.11**).

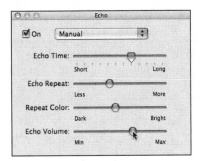

Figure 10.8 The settings window for the echo effect.

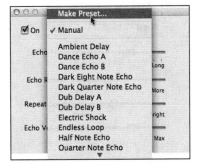

Figure 10.9 The Make Preset command is at the very top of the effects presets pop-up menu.

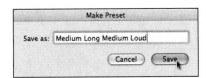

Figure 10.10 Name your new preset.

Figure 10.11 There's your preset on the presets pop-up menu.

Figure 10.12 The checked preset will be deleted.

Figure 10.13 Choosing the Delete Preset command.

Figure 10.14 If you're sure that you want to delete the preset, click Remove.

To delete a preset:

1. Working in the effect's settings window, choose the preset you want to delete (**Figure 10.12**).

2. From the presets pop-up menu, choose Delete Preset (**Figure 10.13**).

3. In the confirmation dialog that appears, click Remove (**Figure 10.14**).

   The preset is removed from the menu.

Saving Instrument Presets

Any changes you make to settings in the Details pane of the Track Info window are considered changes to the instrument assigned to that track. You can save your customized effect settings as a new instrument preset. By default, your new preset will be saved in the same category as the instrument you started with. You can save your new instrument preset in a different category by clicking the category in the left column of the upper part of the Track Info window. Choosing a different category won't affect the actual sound of your instrument; the categories merely help to keep the instruments organized.

To save an instrument preset:

1. If you want to save a preset to a different category, click that category's name in the list in the top half of the Track Info window (**Figure 10.15**).

2. Click the Save Instrument button at the bottom right of the Track Info window (**Figure 10.16**).

3. In the Save As field in the Save Instrument dialog that opens, type a name for the new instrument and click Save (**Figure 10.17**).

   The new preset is added to the instrument list in the Track Info window (**Figure 10.18**).

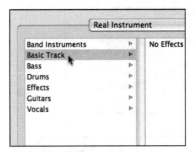

Figure 10.15 If you want, choose a different category in which to save your new instrument preset.

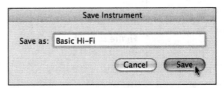

Figure 10.16 The Save Instrument button.

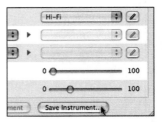

Figure 10.17 The Save Instrument dialog.

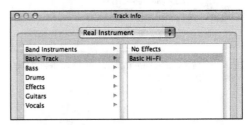

Figure 10.18 Your new preset appears in the top half of the Track Info window.

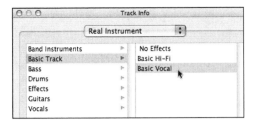

Figure 10.19 Mark an instrument preset for deletion.

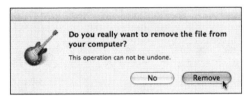

Figure 10.20 The Delete Instrument button.

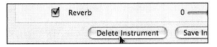

Figure 10.21 You're given one last chance to change your mind.

To delete an instrument preset:

1. Working in the instrument list in the top half of the Track Info window, select the instrument you want to delete (**Figure 10.19**).

2. Click the Delete Instrument button at the bottom left of the window (**Figure 10.20**).

3. In the confirmation dialog that appears, click Remove (**Figure 10.21**).

   The instrument is deleted from the Track Info window list.

✔ Tips

- You can delete only user-created instruments. The instrument presets that ship with GarageBand and the GarageBand Jam Pack cannot be removed.

- The procedures in these tasks can also be used to save and delete master track presets. When you work with the Track Info window for the master track, every occurrence of the word *instrument* on a button or in a dialog is replaced by the word *master*.

The Confusing "Do You Want to Save the File?" Dialog

Often when working in the Track Info window, you will encounter a puzzling dialog (**Figure 10.22**). It can be puzzling for several reasons:

◆ It says that you're changing from one file to another, when all you thought you were doing was switching from one preset to another.

◆ The same message appears whether you change to a different effects preset or to a different instrument preset.

◆ It's triggered when you switch from the Manual effect setting to a saved preset, even if you didn't make any changes to the customized setting.

The bewilderment is caused partly by the fact that GarageBand saves each effect preset and instrument preset as a separate file in the folder /Library/Application Support/GarageBand/ Instrument Library (**Figure 10.23**). Effects and Software Instrument generator presets (which bear the suffix .pst) are collected in folders named for the effects themselves:

Instrument Library/Plug-in Settings/[*name of effect*]

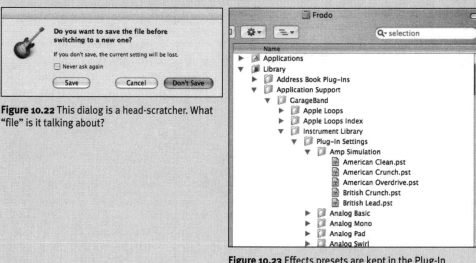

Figure 10.22 This dialog is a head-scratcher. What "file" is it talking about?

Figure 10.23 Effects presets are kept in the Plug-In Settings folder.

The Confusing "Do You Want to Save the File?" Dialog *(continued)*

Instrument presets (bearing the suffix .cst) are located in the Track Settings folder and grouped in subfolders that match the presets' classification in the Track Info window (**Figure 10.24**).

The dialog is somewhat misleading, because it implies that, when working with effects, if you switch from the Manual setting to a saved preset, you will lose your customizations. This is not true. The Manual setting retains your customized settings until you change them yourself. Even if you save and close the song, the next time you open it, the Manual effects setting will be intact. The dialog is merely trying to remind you that your customization hasn't been saved as a preset.

If you want to save your special setting as a preset, go ahead and click Save. If you are changing effects settings, you will be presented with the Save Preset dialog, which works like the Make Preset dialog (Figure 10.10). If you are changing to a different instrument preset, the Save Instrument (or Save Master) dialog will appear (Figure 10.17).

Or you can check the Never Ask Again box to turn off the nagging. With that box checked, it's up to you to remember to save as presets the customizations you want to keep.

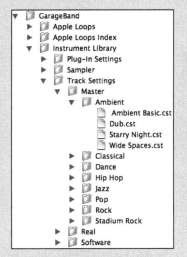

Figure 10.24 Instrument presets are stored in the Track Settings folder.

Using the Echo Effect

Echo is one of the most basic effects. The echo effect causes the source sound to repeat after a delay. To use echo, you must first make sure that it's turned on and choose a setting in the master track Track Info window (echo and the reverb effect share this restriction). Then open the Track Info window for each instrument track to which you want to add echo and enable it there. Use the master track to set the maximum amount of echo in the song; then use the sliders in the Track Info windows for the individual instrument tracks to choose the portion of that maximum you want in each track. Echo has the following parameters (**Figure 10.25**):

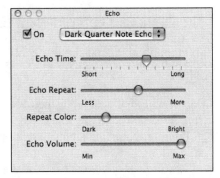

Figure 10.25 Drag these sliders to fine-tune the settings for the echo effect.

◆ **Echo Time:** Adjusts the length of the delay between the original sound and the echo.

◆ **Echo Repeat:** Adjusts the number of times the echo repeats. If you drag the slider all the way to the More end, the echo keeps repeating for a very long time. This echoing can build up and cause feedback if you're not careful.

◆ **Repeat Color:** Changes the tone color of the echo compared with the original sound. Moving the slider toward the Dark end of the scale makes the echo muffled and indistinct, while moving it to the Bright end makes the echo sound tinny and thin. Setting the slider in the middle gives you a nice balance between the two.

◆ **Echo Volume:** Adjusts the volume of the echo relative to the original sound. Dragging the slider toward Min makes the echo softer, and dragging toward Max makes it louder. Remember that you can also control the amount of echo in the individual instrument tracks, so don't set this level too low.

Figure 10.26 The echo effect has been enabled for this song.

Figure 10.27 This slider sets the amount of echo that will be applied to this track.

To use the echo effect:

1. Open the Track Info window for the master track and click the Details pane to reveal the effects controls.

2. Click the Echo check box to turn on the echo effect for the song (**Figure 10.26**).

3. Choose a setting from the presets pop-up menu or click the Edit button and choose your own settings.

4. With the Track Info window still open, select a track in the timeline to which you want to apply the echo effect.

5. Make sure the Echo box is checked and then drag the slider to determine how much of the effect from the master track is applied to the instrument track (**Figure 10.27**).

USING THE ECHO EFFECT

Using the Reverb Effect

Reverb is short for *reverberation*, which is what happens to sound in an enclosed space. The sound bounces off the surfaces of the space, decaying a bit at each bounce. It's like a long, smeared-out echo, without any distinct repetition of the original sound. A judicious amount of reverb can sweeten any recording. It creates a sort of acoustic glow that can create just the right atmosphere for a song, and it can cover up some of the imperfections in a mediocre performance. In the real world, reverberation depends on the size and shape of the room and the materials the walls and ceiling are made from. GarageBand's reverb effect can mimic the reverberation you would hear in a variety of real performing spaces.

Like the echo effect, reverb must be turned on in the master track before it can be applied to any instrument track. Use the master track to set the upper limit for the amount of reverb in the song; then use the sliders in the Track Info windows for the individual instrument tracks to choose how much reverb you want in each track. These are the parameters for reverb (**Figure 10.28**):

◆ **Reverb Time:** Adjusts the length of time it takes for the reverberation to die out completely.

◆ **Reverb Color:** Changes the tone color of the reverberation compared with the original sound. Moving the slider toward the Dark end of the scale favors the low frequencies by making the high frequencies die out faster, while moving it toward the Bright end favors the high frequencies.

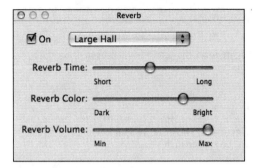

Figure 10.28 These sliders define the characteristics of the reverb effect that will be applied in this song.

Figure 10.29 Reverb has been turned on for this song and a preset has been chosen.

Figure 10.30 Reverb will be applied to this track at about half the intensity defined for the master track.

◆ **Reverb Volume:** Adjusts the volume of the reverb relative to the original sound. At the Max setting, the reverb starts at the same volume as the original sound before beginning to decay. Dragging the slider toward Min causes the reverb to start at lower volumes.

To use the reverb effect:

1. Open the Track Info window for the master track and click the Details pane to reveal the effects controls.

2. Click the Reverb check box to turn on the reverb effect for the song (**Figure 10.29**).

3. Choose a setting from the presets pop-up menu or click the Edit button and choose your own settings.

4. With the Track Info window still open, select a track in the timeline to which you want to apply the reverb effect.

5. Make sure the Reverb box is checked and drag the slider to determine how much of the reverb from the master track is applied to the instrument track (**Figure 10.30**).

Turn Off Effects You're not Using

Some GarageBand users have reported that dragging an effect's slider to 0 is not the same as turning it off—that is, just having echo or reverb enabled appears to sap some of your computer's processing power, even if the values are set to 0. If you are having trouble getting your song to play on your machine, try unchecking any effects you're not actually using. You may free up enough processor cycles to let your song be heard in all its glory. If you're not using echo or reverb on any of your tracks, turning it off on the Master Track saves you the trouble of disabling it on every instrument track.

Using the Equalizer Effect

The equalizer effect (often referred to as EQ) allows you to increase or decrease the volume of different parts of the audio spectrum. To bring out a bass line, for instance, you might boost the low-frequency part of the spectrum, while to make percussion sizzle, you might boost the high frequencies (or treble). Alternatively, if one of your tracks has an annoying rumble or other low-frequency noise, you can cut the bass to try to diminish it.

When applied to individual tracks, the equalizer effect is a helpful tool in the mixing process. Each instrument has a distinctive sound color, which is created by a unique mixture of sounds of various frequencies. But if you have tracks with several different sounds overlapping at once, the different colors are likely to merge into a sort of gray cloud. Use the equalizer effect to increase the color contrast among the different instruments in your song to open up the texture and make it more transparent. A good way to learn about equalization is to experiment with the presets provided with GarageBand. The name of each gives a clear idea of what it's designed to do.

The equalizer settings for each instrument track are independent of the master track setting. Each of the three gain sliders controls a different range of frequencies (**Figure 10.31**). Drag each slider to the left to weaken the frequencies in that range, and drag to the right to strengthen them.

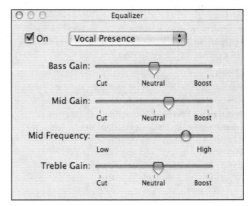

Figure 10.31 Use these sliders to set the equalizer parameters for a song or for a single track.

Figure 10.32 The equalizer effect will be applied to this track.

The Mid Frequency slider lets you pick the range affected by the Mid Gain slider. This range is singled out for special treatment because this is the range to which the human ear is most sensitive. The main notes of melodies and most voices fall in this range. For example, when using the equalizer with the main vocal track in your song, drag the Mid Gain slider to the right (while the track is playing) and then adjust the Mid Frequency slider until the vocal line acquires prominence without becoming shrill or distorted.

◆ **Bass Gain:** Adjusts the strength of low-frequency sounds.

◆ **Mid Gain:** Adjusts the strength of mid-range frequencies, as determined by the Mid Frequency slider.

◆ **Mid Frequency:** Determines the specific part of the middle range of frequencies affected by the Mid Gain slider.

◆ **Treble Gain:** Adjusts the strength of high-frequency sounds.

To use the equalizer:

1. Open the Track Info window for the track to which you want to apply the equalizer effect and click the Details pane to reveal the effects controls.

2. Click the Equalizer check box to enable this effect (**Figure 10.32**).

3. Choose a setting from the presets pop-up menu or click the Edit button and choose your own settings.

Using the Compressor Effect

The compressor effect reduces the dynamic range of a track (or of a song, if applied to the master track). It's especially useful for individual tracks that have a wider dynamic range than the rest of the song: for example, a vocal track that gets extremely soft in places and very loud in others. Such a track is very difficult to balance with other tracks, because if you boost its lowest volume so it can be heard above the rest of the song, its loudest passages will cause distortion (not to mention deafness!).

You can fix this by applying the compressor to the track to reduce the difference between the softest and loudest parts of the song. You might apply compression to an entire song if you knew it was going to be played back on a device with limited dynamic range, such as any portable music player with earbuds.

The compressor setting in the instrumental tracks is independent of the setting in the master track.

To use the compressor effect:

1. Open the Track Info window for the track to which you want to apply the compressor effect and click the Details pane to reveal the effects controls.

2. Click the Compressor check box to enable this effect (**Figure 10.33**).

3. Drag the slider to the right to increase the amount of compression applied to the track, or drag to the left to reduce the amount.

Figure 10.33 The compressor effect will be applied to this track.

Figure 10.34 The check box turns on the gate effect, and the slider specifies the cutoff volume.

Using the Gate Effect

The gate effect is a simple filter that stops sounds below a certain volume from being heard. It can be useful for blocking quiet background noises that intrude upon audio recordings such as the buzz of an amplifier or a guitar pickup.

The gate effect can be applied only to Real Instrument tracks.

To use the gate effect:

1. Open the Track Info window for the Real Instrument track to which you want to apply the gate effect and click the Details pane to reveal the effects controls.

2. Click the Gate check box to enable this effect (**Figure 10.34**).

3. Drag the slider to the right to raise the minimum volume allowed through the gate. Drag the slider to the left to lower the minimum volume allowed.

   A setting of 100 filters out all sound. A low setting allows all but the quietest sounds through, and a setting of 0 admits all sounds.

USING THE GATE EFFECT

About the Other GarageBand Effects

In addition to the basic effects already discussed, GarageBand includes another dozen effects, listed as GarageBand Effects in the top half of the pop-up menus on the left side of the Details pane of the Track Info window (**Figure 10.35**). (I'll touch briefly on the Audio Unit Effects listed in the bottom half of those menus a little later, in "About Audio Units.")

You can apply one of the effects from this menu to the master track; instrument tracks generously provide two identical effects menus per track. Keep in mind that every effect you use adds to the load on your computer's processing power, so unless you have a powerful Mac, use effects sparingly. To add one of these effects to your song, see "To apply effects to a track" earlier in the chapter.

Complete explanations of these effects would be highly technical and are beyond the scope of this book; you can learn a great deal by trying the presets and experimenting with the sliders for each effect. However, since Apple's documentation for GarageBand passes over these effects in silence, here are thumbnail descriptions of each:

◆ **Treble Reduction:** As its name implies, this effect lowers the volume of frequencies in the treble (or high) range. Use it to rid a poorly engineered recording of hiss or to tone down any track that seems shrill. You can also use it in conjunction with reverb to make an instrument seem more distant. Use the Frequency slider to choose the portion of the track's high frequencies that are attenuated. Drag the Frequency slider to the right to affect only the very highest frequencies. Drag it to the left to affect a wider range of frequencies (**Figure 10.36**).

Figure 10.35 The contents of the effects pop-up menu.

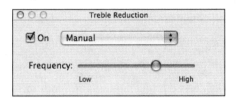

Figure 10.36 The Treble Reduction control.

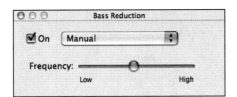

Figure 10.37 The Bass Reduction control.

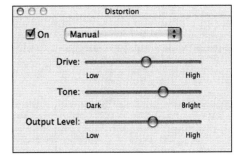

Figure 10.38 The Distortion controls.

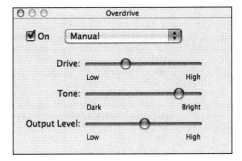

Figure 10.39 The Overdrive controls.

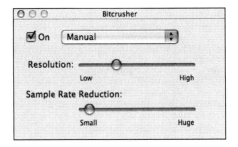

Figure 10.40 The Bitcrusher controls.

◆ **Bass Reduction:** This effect cuts the volume of frequencies in the bass (or low) range. Use this filter to get rid of low-frequency noises that afflict live recording or to attenuate excessively boomy bass instruments or drums. It is also effective for thinning guitars and percussion instruments so they don't muddy the mix as much. Use the Frequency slider to choose the portion of the track's low frequencies that are attenuated. Drag the Frequency slider to the left to affect only the lowest frequencies. Drag it to the right to affect a wider range of frequencies (**Figure 10.37**).

◆ **Distortion:** This effect mimics the crackling, grating sound (some would say "noise") created when a stronger signal is sent through an audio circuit than it can handle. Electric guitars often have pedal-operated distortion modules; add this effect to your electric guitar tracks or use it to make an acoustic guitar sound electric (**Figure 10.38**). Warning: It takes only a little bit of this effect to send your song into clipping territory! Use the track's volume level slider to bring the signal down to a manageable level.

◆ **Overdrive:** This is another effect that imitates the sound of an audio circuit pushed beyond its limits. Overdrive is a kinder, gentler relative of distortion (**Figure 10.39**).

◆ **Bitcrusher:** A purely digital distortion module, the bitcrusher lets you create bizarre effects (**Figure 10.40**). Digital distortion is harsher and more unpleasant than the other distortion modules, but it does have its place. Try out the presets and then experiment on your own.

continues on next page

ABOUT THE OTHER GARAGEBAND EFFECTS

◆ **Automatic Filter:** The automatic filter creates special effects by filtering out high frequencies (set by the Frequency slider) and setting the filtering frequency to resonate with itself (set by the Resonance slider). This resonance manifests itself as a wobble or wah in the sound, whose intensity and speed are controlled by two more sliders (**Figure 10.41**).

◆ **Chorus:** The chorus effect layers copies of the original sound over itself. The copies are slightly delayed in time compared to the original, making it sound like several instruments or voices are performing the same part together (**Figure 10.42**). Use this effect to thicken a track and make it stand out in the mix.

◆ **Flanger:** The flanger effect is similar to the chorus effect, but more extreme. You can achieve some wild effects with the flanger (**Figure 10.43**).

◆ **Phaser:** Another relative of the flanger and chorus effects, the phaser plays the copies of the original sound later in time and also out of phase with the original (that is, the peaks and troughs of its waveforms do not coincide with those of the original). The effect makes the track sound like it is pulsating or whooshing back and forth (**Figure 10.44**).

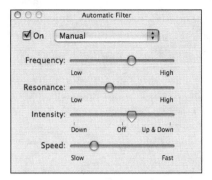

Figure 10.41 The Automatic Filter controls.

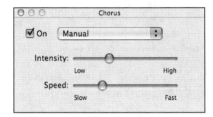

Figure 10.42 The Chorus controls.

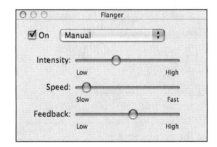

Figure 10.43 The Flanger controls.

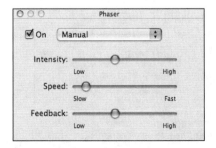

Figure 10.44 The Phaser controls.

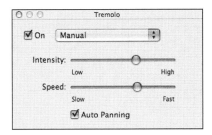

Figure 10.45 The Tremolo controls.

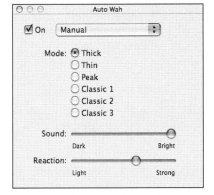

Figure 10.46 The Auto Wah controls.

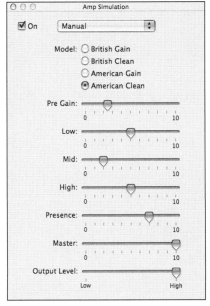

Figure 10.47 The Amp Simulation controls.

◆ **Tremolo:** The tremolo effect adds *vibrato*, a wavering quality, to the sound. Check the Auto Panning box to have the sound bounce back and forth between the left and right stereo channels (**Figure 10.45**).

◆ **Auto Wah:** In the physical world, an auto wah is a device (usually pedal controlled) that converts a change in volume to a change in color. For example, when attached to an electric guitar, it can translate each pluck of a string into a sort of vowel sound (*wah*); changing the intensity of the pluck changes the vowel sound, or color, of the note. GarageBand's auto wah effect is meant to imitate this device (**Figure 10.46**).

◆ **Amp Simulation:** This effect makes your track sound like it has been connected to an electric guitar amplifier. This effect is especially useful when recording an electric guitar through a direct connection to your Mac, bypassing the guitar's own amp. Indeed, all of the Real Instrument guitar settings, and most of the Software Instrument guitar setting, include amp simulation. But it's not just for guitars; this effect works on any instrument, allowing you to play any of your tracks through a virtual guitar amp (**Figure 10.47**).

Editing Software Instruments

For Software Instruments, the Details pane of the Track Info window contains one more item: the Generator pop-up menu, with its attendant presets pop-up menu (**Figure 10.48**). These two menus don't define an effect; rather, they define the instrumental sound of a Software Instrument track.

The checked item on the Generator menu is the basic source of the sound for the instrument. The generators in the top part of the list (Piano through Drum Kits) produce their sounds from recordings, or samples, of actual instruments. The rest of the generators (from Electric Piano on down) rely on synthesized sounds, meaning that GarageBand creates their sound entirely through mathematical calculations.

Your generator choice defines the instrument's basic characteristics. To get a specific instrumental sound, you need to choose a setting from the Generator presets menu. For sampled instruments, the generator acts as a basic model of the instrument in software. When you choose a preset from the Generator presets menu, you tell GarageBand to use a specific folder of samples (bearing the same name as the preset) to create the actual sound of the instrument. These samples reside in /Library/Application Support/GarageBand/Instrument Library/Sampler/Sampler Files.

This presets menu works differently from the effects presets menus in GarageBand. In those menus, a preset is a saved combination of the settings chosen in the effect's settings window. The settings for a generator always consist of the adjustments you make in the settings window *in addition to* the information contained in one of the presets that ships with GarageBand. These factory

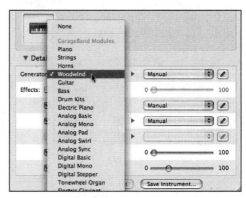

Figure 10.48 The Track Info window showing the Generator pop-up menu.

Factory presets used as the basis for these custom settings

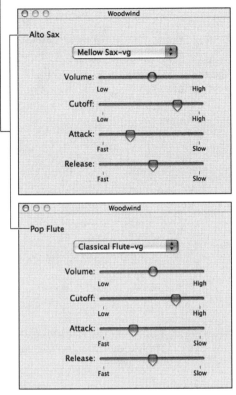

Figure 10.49 Settings windows for two custom instruments based on the Woodwind generator. The slider positions in each are almost identical, but the instruments sound very different, because they are based on different factory presets.

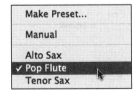

Figure 10.50 The factory presets for the Woodwind generator.

presets can be neither edited nor deleted (because they are tied to a folder of instrument samples); you can create your own presets, but they will always be based on one of the factory presets.

Here's an example: **Figure 10.49** shows the settings windows for two different instrument presets I created using the Woodwind generator. The sliders in both windows are in exactly the same positions; but even so, the two instruments sound very different. That's because I based each of my presets on a different factory preset, so that each of my presets draws upon a different set of sampled files (**Figure 10.50**). The settings window for any Software Instrument using a sample-based generator always displays the name of the factory preset that the current settings are based on.

For synthesizer-based generators, editing presets is much more straightforward. The parameters shown in the settings window are the only adjustments available for the generator, so the presets that come with GarageBand have no greater importance than presets you create.

✔ Tip

■ Just in case you decide to check up on my work and poke around in the Sample Files folder, you'll see that there's one folder of samples whose name doesn't match the corresponding preset: for some reason (just to keep life interesting, I suppose), the files for the Pop Horn Section preset are stored in the Pop Brass Section folder.

To edit a Software Instrument:

1. Select a Software Instrument track whose instrument you want to edit.

2. Open the Track Info window and *do any of the following:*

   ▲ To change to a completely different instrumental sound, choose a new generator from the Generator pop-up menu (Figure 10.48); then choose a preset from the Generator presets pop-up menu (**Figure 10.51**).

   ▲ To make a less drastic change in the instrument's sound, leave the generator alone and choose a preset from the Generator presets pop-up menu (Figure 10.51).

   ▲ To make a subtle change in the instrument's sound, click the Edit button and adjust the controls in the settings window (**Figure 10.52**). Save your settings as a preset, if desired.

3. Click the Save Instrument button at the bottom of the window to save your edited instrument (see "To save an instrument preset" earlier in this chapter).

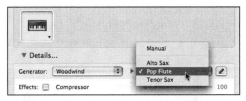

Figure 10.51 The presets pop-up menu for the Woodwind generator.

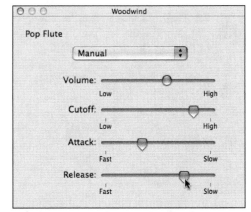

Figure 10.52 The settings window for the Woodwind generator. This example shows a customized setting based on the Pop Flute preset.

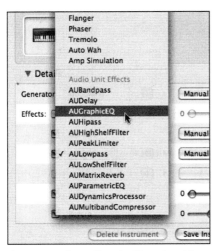

Figure 10.53 The Audio Unit effects that ship with GarageBand.

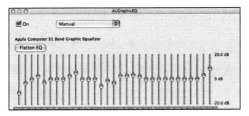

Figure 10.54 The interface for the AUGraphicEQ Audio Unit.

Table 10.1

Audio Unit Equivalents of Standard GarageBand Effects	
AUDIO UNIT	STANDARD EFFECT
AUDelay	Echo
AUMatrixReverb	Reverb
AUGraphicEQ	Equalizer
AUParametricEQ	
AUMultibandCompressor	Compressor
AULowpass	Treble reduction
AUHighShelfFilter	
AUHpass	Bass reduction
AULowShelfFilter	

About Audio Units

Software effects are often distributed as *plug-ins* so they can be loaded into the program on an as-needed basis. To facilitate the sharing of plug-ins among music applications, several standardized plug-in formats have been established. As part of the specification for Mac OS X, Apple introduced yet another plug-in format, the *Audio Unit*. The Audio Unit format is attractive to music software developers because, unlike other plug-in formats, it is supported at the system level, which enables programmers to very easily create music applications compatible with it.

GarageBand, being an Apple product, supports the Audio Unit format and comes with a number of Audio Unit effects. You'll find them listed in the bottom half of the effects pop-up menus (**Figure 10.53**). GarageBand also (in theory) accepts third-party Audio Units. Anecdotal evidence from users indicates that not all Audio Unit plug-ins work with GarageBand, but the majority do.

Many of GarageBand's built-in Audio Units are more complex versions of the program's standard effects. Compare, for example, the interface for the standard equalizer effect, with its three frequency ranges (Figure 10.31), with that for AUGraphicEQ, a plug-in that also functions as an equalizer (**Figure 10.54**). The AUGraphicEQ effect breaks the audio spectrum into a whopping 31 frequency ranges. **Table 10.1** lists some other Audio Units that can substitute for standard GarageBand effects.

Explaining the operation of all of the included Audio Units is beyond the scope of this book. M. Danielson has written a fine tutorial on the use of the Audio Unit effects that are supplied with GarageBand. You'll find it on the Web at www.macjams.com; the title of the article is "GarageBand Tutorial: Built-in Audio Unit Effects".

Using Audio Unit Instrument Plug-Ins

Not all Audio Units are effects plug-ins; there are also Audio Unit instrument plug-ins. AU instruments work like the Software Instrument generators that are included with GarageBand. GarageBand comes with only one such AU instrument plug-in, DLSMusicDevice, which is a very basic component that lets GarageBand access the instrument library built into QuickTime (**Figure 10.55**). There is no documentation for it, and its operation is flaky at best, so I don't recommend it for general use.

There are many third-party AU instrument plug-ins, and most (but not all) seem to work as expected in GarageBand. Normally, they are provided with an installer program; simply run the installer to add the plug-in to your collection. Some plug-ins, however, need to be installed by hand, using the following procedure:

1. Quit GarageBand, if it's running.

2. Open the folder containing the Audio Unit you wish to install (**Figure 10.56**).

3. Locate the item with the suffix *.component* and drag it to the folder /Library/Audio/ Plug-Ins/Components (**Figure 10.57**).

4. Restart GarageBand. The Audio Unit will now be ready for use.

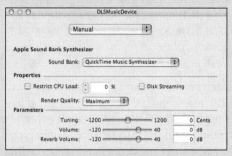

Figure 10.55 The settings window for the DLSMusicService plug-in.

Figure 10.56 The Finder icon for buzZer, a plug-in by alphakanal multimedia gmbh that emulates an analog synthesizer.

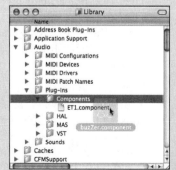

Figure 10.57 Drag-installing the buzZer.component file.

Using Audio Unit Instrument Plug-Ins *(continued)*

Once it's installed, use an AU instrument just like you would any other generator:

1. Select the Software Instrument track in which you want to use the Audio Unit instrument and open the Track Info window.

2. From the Generator menu, choose the AU instrument you want to use (**Figure 10.58**).

3. If the instrument's settings window doesn't open automatically, click the Edit button to open it (**Figure 10.59**).

4. Adjust the plug-in's settings to taste.

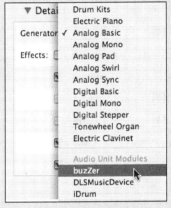

Figure 10.58 Choosing buzZer from the Generator menu.

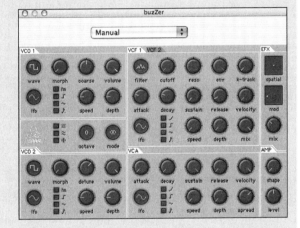

Figure 10.59 The buzZer settings window.

MIXING YOUR SONG

Mixing is the final part of the process of creating a song in GarageBand. You've brought together all of the musical materials you want to use, you've arranged them into just the right sequence, and now it's time to add the finishing touches that make the song come alive.

Mixing a song involves some or all of these tasks:

◆ Setting volume levels for individual tracks so the various instruments balance each other.

◆ Adding volume curves to tracks to create changes in volume over time.

◆ Setting the pan position for each track

◆ Using the master track volume curve to adjust the overall dynamics for the song.

◆ Adjusting the master volume slider so the loudest passages barely turn the master level meters red.

Choosing a Volume Level for Each Track

The fundamental activity in creating a final mix is setting the output volume level of each track. This process has two goals:

◆ To achieve just the right balance among all the different sounds in your song.

◆ To prevent the total output of all tracks from reaching a level high enough to cause distortion, or *clipping*.

Achieving balance

In your song, you want the percussion to have real punch and the bass line to have presence, but you also want to ensure that the combination of all the parts doesn't swamp the melody line. You can use the volume level sliders to cut back the levels of accompanying tracks to let the more important tracks shine. If you have an instrument that stays mostly in the background but steps forward for one eight-bar solo (a guitarist, for example), add a volume curve to that instrument's track. You can use the volume curve to lower the track's level for most of the song, but then boost the volume during the instrument's time in the spotlight. Likewise, if your singer has problems with breath control and can't maintain an even dynamic level, you can use a volume curve to compensate.

Preventing clipping

In Chapter 6, I stressed the importance of watching individual track levels while recording to keep the track from clipping (see "About Setting the Recording Level" in Chapter 6). Even if you scrupulously monitor each track and none of them reaches clipping level, you still may find that when all of the tracks in your song are played together, clipping occurs.

Figure 11.1 The master level meters, showing clipping in progress. Use the master volume slider, just below the meters, to adjust the output level of the song.

To monitor clipping in the song as a whole, watch the master level meters in the lower-right corner of the GarageBand window (see "Setting the Output Volume" later in this chapter). Like the individual track level meters, they include clipping indicators that turn red when clipping occurs (**Figure 11.1**).

There are several possible causes for clipping, and for each cause there is a remedy:

◆ If several of your tracks remain at a high volume throughout, use their respective volume level sliders to reduce their overall levels (see "Setting the Volume Level for a Track" later in this chapter).

◆ If two or more tracks have simultaneous loud passages, add volume level curves to those tracks and back off the volume during those passages (see "About Track Volume Curves" later in this chapter).

◆ If you're sure you've found the perfect balance among all of your tracks and you don't want to adjust one or two of them to get rid of clipping, use the master volume slider to lower the output level of the whole song (see "Setting the Output Volume" later in this chapter).

◆ If you added effects to some of your tracks, the effects may have boosted the tracks' volume enough to cause clipping. Open the Track Info window for each of those tracks and reduce the strength of the applied effects (see Chapter 10), or reduce the track's volume.

Setting levels for each track in a song and then a final output level for the entire song is not a linear process. You set individual track levels, then adjust the master volume slider, then perhaps open the Track Info window and tweak the effects for a track or two, then adjust the master volume slider again, and so on. The ultimate guide in this process is your own musical taste. Keep fiddling with the controls until the song sounds right.

Setting the Volume Level for a Track

Use the volume slider in the track mixer to set the basic volume level for a track. Later, I'll show you how to program volume changes into a track, so some sections play more loudly or softly than others (see "About Track Volume Curves" later in this chapter).

Figure 11.2 Clicking the triangle reveals the Mixer column.

Figure 11.3 Drag the track volume slider to adjust its output level.

To set a track's volume level:

1. If the track mixer is hidden, click the triangle at the top right of the Tracks column (Command-Y).

   The track mixer appears (**Figure 11.2**).

2. Drag the volume slider right to increase the track's volume level, or left to decrease it (**Figure 11.3**).

   Continue to the next track and set its level, until you have taken care of all the tracks in your song.

✔ Tip

- All of the volume sliders in GarageBand are set by default to their neutral position, meaning that they cause neither an increase nor a decrease in volume, or *gain*. This setting is also called "0 dB gain," because the gain is adjusted by 0 dB. The term *dB* is the abbreviation for *decibel*, a unit of sound intensity. To reset the volume level slider to its neutral position, Option-click the slider (see "Using the Track Mixer Volume Slider" in Chapter 6).

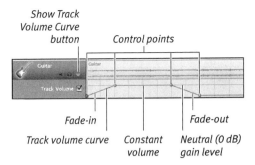

Show Track Volume Curve button

Control points

Track volume curve   Constant volume   Neutral (0 dB) gain level

Fade-in   Fade-out

Figure 11.4 A simple track volume curve showing a fade-in and a fade-out.

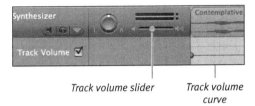

Track volume slider   Track volume curve

Figure 11.5 This is how the track volume curve looks when first enabled.

✔ Tip

- The term *track volume curve* is a bit of a misnomer, because GarageBand lets you use only straight lines in your "curve" (unlike pricier audio applications, which allow you to draw nice, smooth curves).

About Track Volume Curves

The track mixer volume slider provides an easy way to set the output level for a track, but this method is also inflexible. The level you set is maintained unwaveringly throughout the song. If you add a *volume curve* to a track, on the other hand, you can create volume changes over time, or *fades*. Raising a track's volume level from silence is called a *fade-in*, and bringing it back down to silence is a *fade-out*. A more sophisticated effect is the *crossfade*, in which one track fades in while another track fades out.

Editing track volume curves is much like editing MIDI controller data (see "Editing MIDI Controller Information" in Chapter 9): set control points along the curve at spots where you want the volume to change; then drag each point up and down to adjust the volume at that location. GarageBand automatically adjusts the curve to follow your control points (**Figure 11.4**). Parts of the curve that slope upward to the right represent increases in volume, or *crescendos*; parts that slope downward to the right represent decreases in volume, or *decrescendos*.

You can add a volume curve to any track. Doing so disables that track's volume slider. You can also add a volume curve to the master track to make volume changes that apply to the song as a whole (see "Working with the Master Track Volume Curve" later in this chapter).

When you first display a track volume curve, it is dimmed to show that it's disabled. When enabled for the first time, the curve appears as a straight purple line at the level corresponding to the current track volume slider setting (**Figure 11.5**). The curve also initially has a single control point at its left end. Drag this control point up and down to adjust the overall volume for the track (this is equivalent to adjusting the volume slider).

Editing a Track Volume Curve

If you don't want a track's volume to remain constant throughout a song, add control points to the track wherever you want volume changes to begin or end. Editing track volume curves is much like editing MIDI controller data (see "Editing MIDI Controller Information" in Chapter 9). You can drag control points up or down to adjust the volume level, and left or right to move them to different points in time. You can select control points so you can change several at once, and you can copy, paste, or delete them altogether.

To use a track volume curve:

1. Select the track whose volume curve you want to display.

2. Click the Show Volume Curve button or press A (**Figure 11.6**).

    The track's volume curve pops into view under the track throughout the length of the timeline (**Figure 11.7**).

3. Select the Track Volume check box to enable the track volume curve (**Figure 11.8**).

    When first turned on, the track volume curve is a straight line representing the current value of the track volume slider.

4. Drag the control point at the left end of the curve to set the track's initial volume (**Figure 11.9**).

Figure 11.6 Click this button to reveal the volume curve.

Figure 11.7 The volume curve appears, but is dimmed.

Figure 11.8 The track volume curve is now enabled.

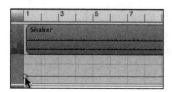

Figure 11.9 The shaker will enter at low volume.

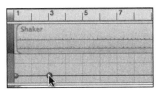

Figure 11.10 Click to place the first control point where you want the fade to begin.

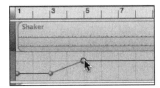

Figure 11.11 Click to place the second control point and drag to the new volume. Here, a fade lasting two measures has been added to the track.

5. Click the track volume curve at a spot where you want the track's volume to start to change (**Figure 11.10**).

A control point is added to the curve.

6. Place another control point at the spot where you want the volume to stop changing; then drag up or down to the new volume (**Figure 11.11**).

7. Continue adding and adjusting control points until you're satisfied with the track's volume changes.

8. To hide the track volume curve, again click the Show Volume Curve control or select the track and press A.

✔ Tips

- The Shaker region goes from dark in Figure 11.9 to light in Figure 11.10 because once you start manipulating the track volume curve, the regions in the track become deselected. The track itself, however, remains selected.

- If you've created a complicated volume curve for a track and you want to hear the track at full volume temporarily, uncheck the Track Volume check box and your volume curve will be disabled. This is useful if you've faded out a portion of a track and you'd like to hear what it sounds like without changing the complex volume curve you just created. When the volume curve is disabled, you can adjust the track volume using the volume slider, but once you enable the volume curve again, the slider will follow the levels set in the volume curve.

Creating a Basic Crossfade

A *crossfade* is a common audio effect: one track fades out as another track fades in. This simple yet sophisticated effect creates a seamless transition from one instrument or musical phrase to another.

Figure 11.12 The first step in making a two-measure crossfade is to create a two-measure overlap between the regions involved.

GarageBand lacks a specific tool for creating crossfades (a common feature in more expensive music programs), but you can easily duplicate the effect with track volume curves. Simply set the control points of one track's volume curve to fade to silence (*fade out*) over a period of time, and use the other track's curve so that the track increases in volume (*fades in*) during the same period.

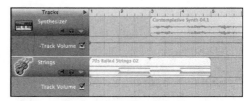

Figure 11.13 The track volume curves are enabled.

To create a crossfade:

1. Make sure the two regions you want to use for the crossfade overlap by at least the amount of time you want the cross-fade to last (**Figure 11.12**).

2. Enable the track volume curves for the two tracks involved in the crossfade by selecting the Track Volume check box for each track (**Figure 11.13**).

3. If your song contains other tracks, you may want to set the tracks involved in the crossfade to Solo mode by clicking each track's Solo button (**Figure 11.14**). This lets you hear the crossfade by itself.

Solo button

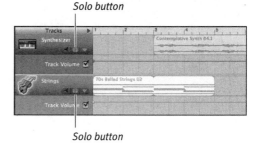

Solo button

Figure 11.14 The tracks are set to Solo mode.

4. Working in the track that will fade out, place a control point on the volume curve at the location where you want the fade to begin (**Figure 11.15**).

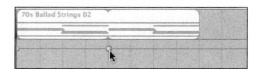

Figure 11.15 The fade-out will start at this control point.

5. Place another control point where you want the fade out to end (**Figure 11.16**).

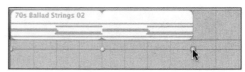

Figure 11.16 The fade-out will end at this control point.

Figure 11.17 The track now fades to silence at the second control point.

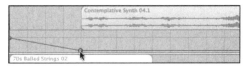

Figure 11.18 The first control point has been dragged down so the fade-in can begin from silence.

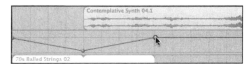

Figure 11.19 At the end of the fade-in, the track is at full volume.

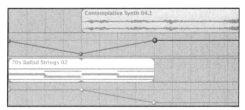

Figure 11.20 The upper track fades in as the lower track fades out.

6. Drag the second control point down as far as it will go (**Figure 11.17**).

At this point, the track will be inaudible. This completes the fade-out.

7. Working in the track that will fade in, place a control point at the location where you want the fade-in to begin; then drag the point down as far as it will go (**Figure 11.18**).

The fade-in will begin from silence.

8. Place another control point at the location where you want the fade-in to end; then drag up to the desired level (**Figure 11.19**).

The crossfade is now complete (**Figure 11.20**).

✔ Tip

■ Note that the left end of the track volume curve in Figure 11.19 rises up to a significant level. In this case, it doesn't disturb our fade-in because that part of the track is empty. If there were a region in the track to the left of the region we wanted to fade in (as there might be if our crossfade were in the middle of a piece), we would probably have to add more control points and adjust more of the track to a lower volume to ensure a silent start to the fade-in.

Setting the Pan Position

Modern stereophonic recording captures the positions of the musicians in the studio relative to each other. When such a recording is played back through two (or more) speakers, the listener hears the performers distributed throughout the aural space, or *stereo field*, which adds a sense of presence and space to the recording.

By default, all of your GarageBand tracks sound like they're centered in front of the listener—a pretty uninteresting mix. Fortunately, you can give each track its own *pan* (for *panorama*) *position* so it has a specific left-to-right placement in the recording's stereo field. Drag the pan wheel in the track mixer to set a track's pan position. The white dot on the perimeter of the wheel shows the track's current pan setting.

Customarily, vocals and drums are positioned more or less centrally, with other percussion instruments and bass placed a short distance either side of center. Guitars and other harmony or melody instruments are then located farther to the left or right. What you are striving for in a good stereo mix is an *overall* balance—there may be moments when there's more going on in the left or right speaker, but the song as a whole should feel balanced in the stereo field.

Drag left or right

Drag up or down

Figure 11.21 The pan wheel reacts differently to dragging depending on where the dragging begins.

Figure 11.22 Clicking at the 3 o'clock position causes the pan wheel to point to the right.

To set a track's pan position:

◆ Display the track mixer if it's not already open; *then do one of the following:*

▲ Place the pointer over the center of the pan wheel and drag down or up to move the track to the right or left, respectively, in the stereo field.

▲ Place the pointer over the outer edge of the pan wheel and drag left or right to move the track to the left or right, respectively. When you use this method, the wheel snaps to each of the white tick marks around the perimeter (**Figure 11.21**).

▲ Click a point around the edge of the wheel to choose a setting (**Figure 11.22**).

✔ Tip

■ Option-click the pan wheel to reset it to the default center position.

Working with the Master Track Volume Curve

To apply effects and to set an overall volume for your song, use the master track (introduced in Chapter 10). The master track not only has its own collection of effects presets, accessible by way of the Track Info window; it also has its own volume curve, which appears at the very bottom of the timeline when the track is displayed (**Figure 11.23**).

The master track's volume curve works just like the volume curves for ordinary tracks (see "About Track Volume Curves" earlier in this chapter). The first time you display the master track for a song, its volume curve is dimmed to show that it is disabled. By default, the curve is a straight line at the neutral (0 dB) gain volume level and represents a constant volume setting for the entire song. If you enable the master volume curve, you can drag it up or down to adjust this constant volume. Alternatively, if you want the dynamics of your song to change from time to time, add control points to the master volume level curve and adjust them up or down. You can use the master track volume curve to end a song with a fade-out, for example.

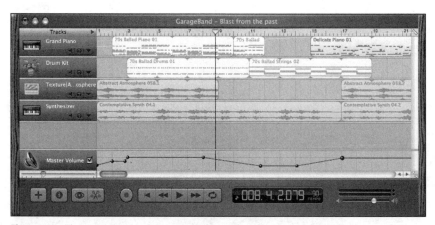

Figure 11.23 The master track volume curve appears at the bottom of the timeline when the master track is displayed.

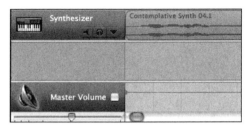

Figure 11.24 The master track's volume curve is inactive by default.

Figure 11.25 The master track volume curve is now ready for action.

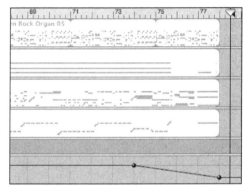

Figure 11.26 The master track volume curve was used to create a fade-out at the end of this song.

To add volume changes to a song:

1. Choose Track > Show Master Track (Command-B).

   The master track is displayed along the bottom of the timeline (**Figure 11.24**). The master track volume curve is dimmed by default.

2. Select the Master Volume check box to enable the master track's volume curve (**Figure 11.25**).

   The volume curve turns purple, indicating that it is ready to be adjusted. The curve has a single control point, located at its extreme left end.

3. Set control points along the master track volume curve and create fade-ins and fade-outs (**Figure 11.26**).

✔ Tip

- To hide the master track, again choose Track > Show Master Track or press Command-B.

THE MASTER TRACK VOLUME CURVE

Setting the Output Volume

The last step you need to take before exporting your song to iTunes is to use the master volume slider to set the song's output level. Even if you've been assiduously tweaking track levels and the master volume curve to rid the song of clipping, listen to the entire song one more time, while keeping a close eye on the master level meters. The master level meters work identically to the individual track level meters and include a clipping indicator that lights up red when clipping is encountered (see "Using the Track Level Meters" in Chapter 6). Adjust the master volume slider until the clipping indicators no longer come on while the song is playing.

To set the output volume for a song:

◆ Play the song from the beginning and watch the track level meters for clipping (**Figure 11.27**); *do one of the following:*

▲ If the clipping indicators light up, drag the master volume slider left to lower the output level until the song no longer clips (**Figure 11.28**).

▲ If the song seems too quiet, drag the master volume slider right to raise the output level. Be sure not to raise it so much that clipping occurs.

Master level meters   *Clipping indicators*

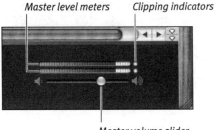

Master volume slider

Figure 11.27 The clipping indicators are illuminated, showing that the output level of the song is too high.

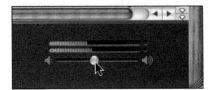

Figure 11.28 Dragging the slider to the left lowers the output volume, preventing clipping.

EXPORTING AND IMPORTING

Sure, it's fun just to play around in GarageBand, but eventually you'll accumulate a repertoire of finished songs. You may want to share some of the fruits of your creative endeavors with friends. Or perhaps your songs are intimate diary musings that you want to keep to yourself, but you want to copy them to your iPod to take with you wherever you go.

And creative work isn't just about output. You may want to assemble pieces of music from bits of sound collected from a variety of sources. Is there any way to bring these nuggets into GarageBand?

GarageBand is extremely limited in its relations with the rest of the world—that's one characteristic that distinguishes it from pricier music programs. But there are a few things you can do to get music into and out of GarageBand. In this chapter I discuss:

◆ Exporting GarageBand songs to iTunes.

◆ Using iTunes to convert songs into more portable formats.

◆ Using GarageBand songs in the other iLife applications.

◆ Importing audio files into GarageBand.

◆ A third-party utility for importing MIDI files into GarageBand.

GarageBand and Other Applications

The only way to turn your GarageBand song into a more portable form is to export it to iTunes. At the moment, anyway, you can't open your GarageBand project in another music program, although Apple has said that a future version of Logic, its high-priced professional music program, will be able to import GarageBand projects.

Likewise, GarageBand can't open project files from other music programs. There's also only one officially sanctioned way of getting pre-existing music into GarageBand (aside from using Apple Loops). You can drag an audio file into GarageBand from the Finder. This creates a new Real Instrument track, which you can treat just as you would treat any Real Instrument track you recorded in GarageBand yourself.

There's also a nifty third-party utility for importing MIDI data into GarageBand; see "Bringing MIDI Files into GarageBand" later in this chapter.

BandToLogic

Enterprising developer Christian Renz is working on a temporary bridge over the GarageBand-Logic gap to help users across until Apple builds its own. His utility, BandToLogic, extracts Logic data from GarageBand project files and saves it as a Logic file. Note that as of this writing, it is still at version 0.1, so it is definitely a work in progress (the author himself refers to it as a "quick hack"). I have not tried it myself; this sidebar is provided for informational purposes only.

If you're feeling brave, download the software from this Web site:

www.web42.com/software/bandtologic/

Exporting a Song to iTunes

One way of sharing your songs with your friends and the world is to hand out your GarageBand file. This gets cumbersome pretty quickly, because anyone who wants to listen to your song has to have a copy of GarageBand and a Mac, and that Mac must be powerful enough to process in real time all the tracks and effects you've included in your composition.

Fortunately, you can also export your songs to iTunes, which is freely available to any Mac or Windows user and has far more modest hardware requirements. Better still, you can use iTunes to compress the exported song file, making it even more portable. And once you've built up a repertoire of immortal compositions, you can use iTunes to burn your works onto a CD.

In addition, all of the songs in your iTunes library are automatically made available to other iLife programs on your Mac, so they can be used as background music in an iPhoto slideshow, an iMovie film, or an iDVD menu or slideshow.

The process of exporting is fairly straight-forward, though not without its pitfalls. The exported song will be placed in a special iTunes playlist, which you choose in GarageBand's Preferences dialog. In the same dialog, you can also choose the names of the composer and album that will be saved with the song.

The exported song file, however, will have the same name as your GarageBand project—GarageBand doesn't let you save the exported file under another name. This becomes awkward if you export the same song more than once. You then end up with a bunch of identically titled songs in your iTunes playlist.

continues on next page

EXPORTING A SONG TO ITUNES

You can give each song a new name in the iTunes library by selecting the song, waiting a second and then clicking the song title, and then typing a new name. And don't worry—if you export a song more than once, a number is appended to the name of the exported file, and this number is incremented each time, so the most recent file doesn't overwrite previous files.

To set export preferences:

1. Choose GarageBand > Preferences (Command-,).

   The Preferences dialog opens.

2. Click the Export button to display the Export pane (**Figure 12.1**).

   By default, GarageBand derives the playlist name, composer name, and album name from the name of the currently logged-in user.

3. If you want to customize these entries, type new names in the fields (**Figure 12.2**).

4. Close the Preferences dialog.

Figure 12.1 Default settings in the Export pane of the GarageBand Preferences dialog.

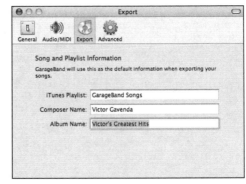

Figure 12.2 Custom names have been entered in some of the fields.

Choosing How Much of Your Song Is Exported

When you create a new song, its length is automatically set to 200 measures (see "About Song Length" in Chapter 2). But if you don't fill up all 200 bars with music, GarageBand doesn't insist on exporting the empty measures along with the occupied ones. By default, when you export a song, GarageBand ends the export after the end of the final region of the song.

You can choose to export a smaller portion of the song by dragging the end-of-song marker to the point where you want the export to end, but note that you can't drag the marker any farther left than measure 32.

Using the end-of-song marker to define the part of the song to be exported works only if the part you want to export begins at the start of the song. If you want to export a portion of the middle of the song, turn on the cycle region (see "Re-recording a Section of a Song" in either Chapter 6 or Chapter 7) and adjust the cycle region to encompass only those measures that you want to export.

Figure 12.3 The Export to iTunes command.

Figure 12.4 The Creating Mixdown progress bar.

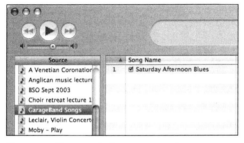

Figure 12.5 The exported song appears in a new playlist in iTunes.

To export a song to iTunes:

1. Choose File > Export to iTunes (**Figure 12.3**).

   The export process begins, and the Creating Mixdown dialog appears (**Figure 12.4**). Click the Cancel button if you want to halt the export process.

   When the progress bar reaches its end and the Creating Mixdown dialog vanishes, the process is complete.

2. Start iTunes.

   Your exported song file will be added to the playlist you specified in GarageBand's preferences. If a playlist with that name didn't exist before, it will be created (**Figure 12.5**).

✔ Tips

■ If you use echo or reverb on one of your tracks, you may find that the last bit of the effect gets cut off when you export your song, because the effect lingers after the final region has been played. To solve this problem, add a new track and drag a loop into the timeline at the end of the song. Loop it so it extends a few measures past the end of the other regions and turn its track volume to zero. When you export the song, GarageBand doesn't stop recording until this region ends, even though the track is inaudible.

■ Many GarageBand users have reported that when they export a song, a file named "Bounced" is unexpectedly produced and ends up in a generic folder in their iTunes library. See "Getting Around the Bounced Bug" in Appendix A for some possible solutions to this vexing problem.

Using iTunes to Compress Your Song

GarageBand exports songs as uncompressed (that is to say, large) *AIFF* (Audio Interchange File Format) files. AIFF is a high-quality format, similar to the format used to store music data on CDs, but AIFF files also have correspondingly large file sizes. This makes AIFF inconvenient as a file sharing medium. You can use iTunes to rip the file to a compressed format, reducing its size by a factor of 10 in the process. You can then e-mail your song to friends, or download it to a portable music player (such as an iPod), or post it on a Web site.

You have a choice of two encoding schemes when exporting songs from iTunes—MP3 and AAC—and for each scheme, you can choose a quality setting. The quality setting has a direct effect on the size of the resulting file: the higher the quality, the bigger the file. AAC produces higher-quality files than MP3 when the files are encoded at the same data rate, but the MP3 format is compatible with a far wider range of players. Use AAC if you are encoding files for your own use or for copying to an iPod, or if you know that the recipients of your files all have QuickTime 6.2 or later installed. For distribution to a wider audience or for copying to MP3 players other than an iPod, use MP3.

Note that iTunes exports files in the same format you choose for importing files, so you (counterintuitively) choose the export format from the Import Using menu in the iTunes Preferences dialog.

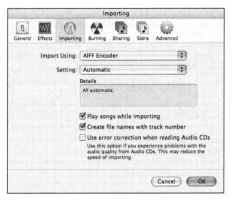

Figure 12.6 The Importing pane of the iTunes Preferences dialog.

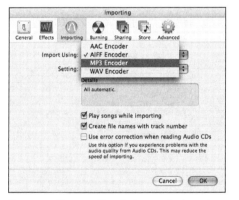

Figure 12.7 The encoding choices on the Import Using menu.

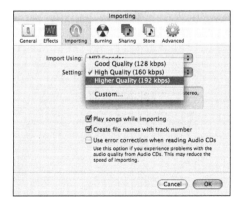

Figure 12.8 The choices on the Setting menu when the MP3 encoder is in use. This menu will look different if you choose another encoder.

The encoding process does not affect your original song file; rather, a new file is created. One slightly annoying feature of the process is that iTunes doesn't keep the encoded file in the same playlist. It just dumps the file into the library with all the rest of your iTunes songs. If you want to keep a song with the rest of the songs you exported from GarageBand, you must put it in the GarageBand playlist manually. One more thing: the encoded file will appear in iTunes lists with the exact same name as the original song, so you'll need to rename one of the files if you want to tell them apart.

To compress your file in iTunes:

1. Choose iTunes > Preferences (Command-,) to open the iTunes Preferences dialog and then click the Importing button.

   The Importing pane appears (**Figure 12.6**).

2. From the Import Using pop-up menu, choose an encoding method (**Figure 12.7**).

3. From the Setting pop-up menu, choose a quality setting (**Figure 12.8**); then click OK to close the dialog.

continues on next page

USING iTUNES TO COMPRESS YOUR SONG

4. Working in the main iTunes window, select the file or files you want to encode (**Figure 12.9**).

5. In the Importing pane, choose Advanced > Convert Selection to [*chosen format*].

A progress bar at the top of the iTunes window tracks the conversion process for each song (**Figure 12.10**). If you want to cancel conversion, click the X to the right of the progress bar.

A tone sounds when the conversion process is complete.

6. Working in the Source list on the left side of the iTunes window, click Library to display all the songs you've added to iTunes and find your newly converted song (**Figure 12.11**).

7. If you wish, rename the converted file and drag it to your GarageBand playlist.

✔ Tips

■ The fourth choice in the Import Using menu is WAV. This is another uncompressed audio format and is the standard audio format in the Windows world. If you want to use your song in a Windows audio program, convert it to WAV first.

■ If you want to convert your song into an Apple Loop (see "Adding More Loops to GarageBand" in Chapter 4), leave the file in AIFF format or convert it to WAV.

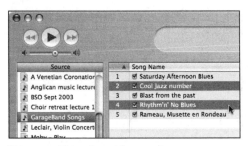

Figure 12.9 Files selected for encoding.

Figure 12.10 The iTunes conversion progress bar.

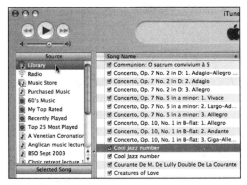

Figure 12.11 The newly converted file joins the original file in your iTunes library.

Slideshow button

Figure 12.12 Use this window to adjust slideshow settings.

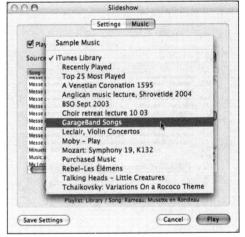

Figure 12.13 Selecting the GarageBand playlist from the Source menu.

Using GarageBand Songs in Other iLife Programs

A great feature of Apple's iLife application suite is the ease with which the programs can share media assets. One of the best examples of this is the ready availability of your entire iTunes library in each application. I can't provide a complete introduction to each program, but I can show you how to access your iTunes library and playlists in the other three applications in iLife '04.

To add a GarageBand song to a slideshow in iPhoto 4

1. Working in the main iPhoto window, select an album in the Source list.

2. Click the Slideshow button to open the Slideshow window (**Figure 12.12**).

3. Click the Music tab to display the Music pane.

4. Choose your GarageBand playlist from the Source pop-up menu (**Figure 12.13**).

5. Choose a song from your GarageBand playlist and *do one of the following:*
    ▲ Click Cancel to close the dialog without saving any settings.
    ▲ Click Play to watch the slideshow with your song playing in the background. Click again to halt playback.
    ▲ Click Save Settings to close the Slideshow window without playing the slideshow.

    Clicking Play or Save Settings preserves your settings for the selected album. When you next play the slideshow for the album, the song you selected will play in the background.

To add a GarageBand song to the soundtrack of an iMovie project:

1. Working in the timeline viewer in the iMovie window, place the playhead in the movie where you want your song to begin playing.

2. Click the Audio button to display the Audio pane (**Figure 12.14**).

3. From the Audio Source pop-up menu, choose your GarageBand playlist (**Figure 12.15**).

4. Click the Place at Playhead button to insert your song into the movie at the playhead's position (**Figure 12.16**).

   When the movie is played, your song will be heard in the soundtrack at the playhead's current position.

Audio Source pop-up menu

Audio pane

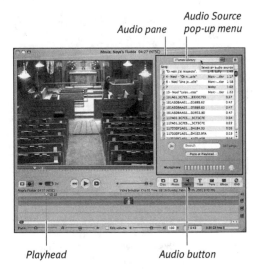

Playhead

Audio button

Figure 12.14 The iMovie window, displaying the Audio pane.

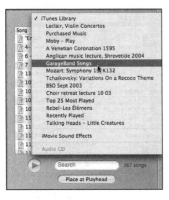

Figure 12.15 Choosing the GarageBand playlist.

Place at Playhead button

GarageBand song inserted into movie

Figure 12.16 The song is added to the movie at the playhead.

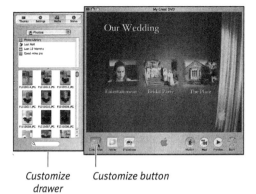

Customize   Customize button
drawer

Figure 12.17 Clicking the Customize button opens the Customize drawer.

Figure 12.18 Choose Audio to display the songs in your iTunes library.

To choose a GarageBand song to play in the background of a DVD menu in iDVD:

1. Working in the main iDVD window, display the menu in which you want your song to play.

2. Click the Customize button to open the Customize drawer (**Figure 12.17**).

3. Click the Media button at the top of the Customize drawer to switch to the Media pane, if it's not already open.

4. Choose Audio from the pop-up menu at the top of the Media pane to display the contents of your iTunes library (**Figure 12.18**).

5. In the top part of the Audio list, click the playlist that contains your GarageBand songs.

   The contents of the playlist are displayed in the bottom part of the Audio list (**Figure 12.19**).

6. Select a song from the playlist to play in the background of the DVD menu.

   When a DVD burned from this project is played, the song you chose will play in the background when this menu is on the screen.

Figure 12.19 The GarageBand playlist.

USING GARAGEBAND SONGS IN iLIFE PROGRAMS

To choose a song to play in the background of an iDVD slideshow:

1. Double-click a slideshow button in the menu currently displayed in iDVD (**Figure 12.20**).

   The slideshow opens in the slideshow editor.

2. Follow steps 1 through 4 of the previous task to display the iTunes playlist containing your GarageBand songs.

3. Drag a song from your playlist to the Audio well at the bottom of the slideshow window (**Figure 12.21**).

4. Click the Return button to close the slideshow editor and return to the previous menu.

   The song will now play in the background during the slideshow.

Slideshow buttons

Figure 12.20 Double-click a slideshow button to open the slideshow editor.

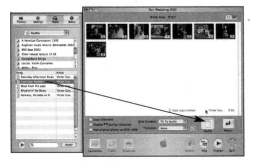

Figure 12.21 Dragging a song to the Audio well.

---

iTunes and iLife Resources

For information about iTunes and the rest of the iLife '04 suite of products, here are some suggestions for further reading (all from Peachpit Press, of course):

iTunes 4 for Macintosh and Windows: Visual QuickStart Guide by Judith Stern and Robert Lettieri.

Apple Training Series: iLife '04 by Michael Rubin.

The Macintosh iLife '04: An Interactive Guide to iTunes, iPhoto, iMovie, iDVD, and GarageBand by Jim Heid.

Robin Williams Cool Mac Apps: A Guide to iLife, Mac.com, and More by Robin Williams and John Tollett.

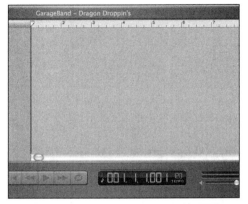

Figure 12.22 These files are ready to be dragged into GarageBand.

Vertical bar; the new region will begin here

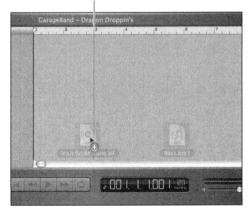

Figure 12.23 The files are poised over the timeline.

Bringing Audio Files into GarageBand

You can add an audio file to your GarageBand song merely by dragging it into the timeline from the Finder. The file can be stored anywhere on your hard disk or on an audio CD inserted into your computer. You can drag the file to an existing Real Instrument track, and the imported file will appear as a new region. The imported file replaces any pre-existing regions that it overlaps. You can also drag the file to the empty area below the tracks already in the song, and a new Real Instrument track will be created for the file. You can drag multiple files at once; each file will be placed in its own track.

This drag-and-drop method of bringing material into GarageBand works for any file in AIFF, WAV, or MP3 format. If you import an MP3 file, GarageBand will convert it to AIFF before adding it to the song. This may take some time, so be prepared to wait.

Caution: If the file you drag into GarageBand was not created by you, be sure to get its author's permission before distributing the song beyond the confines of your own personal computer.

To drag an audio file into GarageBand:

1. In the Finder, locate the file (or files) you want to bring into GarageBand. Arrange your Finder and GarageBand windows so you can see both the file and the GarageBand timeline at the same time (**Figure 12.22**).

2. Drag the file from the Finder into the GarageBand timeline; a vertical bar shows you where the new region will begin (**Figure 12.23**).

continues on next page

BRINGING AUDIO FILES INTO GARAGEBAND

3. When the file is in position, release the mouse button.

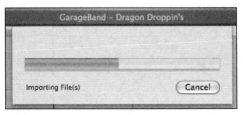

Figure 12.24 The Importing progress bar.

The Importing dialog lets you track the progress of the operation (**Figure 12.24**; if you dragged an MP3 file into the timeline, the dialog says "Converting" instead). If you want, you can click Cancel to stop the procedure.

A new region is added to your song for each file you dragged into the timeline. If you dragged the files over the blank area of the timeline, new tracks are created as well (**Figure 12.25**).

4. If you want, open the track editor and then select each of the new tracks in turn and give them distinctive names.

Figure 12.25 Dragging two files into the GarageBand timeline results in two new tracks.

8-Bit Files Not Allowed

If you drag an audio file into GarageBand but are greeted with the alert shown in **Figure 12.26**, your file was probably created by an antique piece of software. Today, 16-bit resolution is the norm for audio files (largely because it's part of the audio CD standard), and just about every music program expects 16-bit audio files. GarageBand, obviously, insists upon them.

All is not lost, however. You can open the file in Apple's QuickTime Player application, and if you've paid the $30 for QuickTime Pro, you can export it as a 16-bit file.

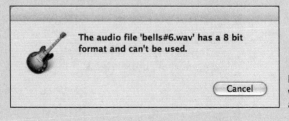

Figure 12.26 You'll encounter this warning if you try to import an 8-bit audio file into GarageBand.

Figure 12.27 The Dent du MIDI application icon.

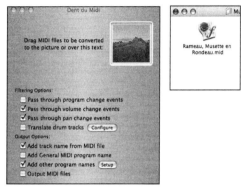

Figure 12.28 Position the Dent du MIDI window near the window that displays the MIDI file.

Figure 12.29 Drag the MIDI file into the Dent du MIDI window.

Bringing MIDI Files into GarageBand

Right out of the box, GarageBand does not allow you to import MIDI files. Fortunately, independent developer Bery Rinaldo created Dent du MIDI, a free utility that converts standard MIDI files into a format that GarageBand understands. Drop a MIDI file onto the Dent du MIDI application icon, and the program outputs a folder containing a set of AIFF files (with the .aif extension). Each file contains the MIDI data from one track in the original file and takes its name from that track. Drag these files into GarageBand's timeline, and each file becomes a new Software Instrument track. The files lack instrument assignments, so you'll need to use the Track Info window to associate an instrument with each one.

I've provided a brief introduction to the software's use. The sample file began as an orchestral score (containing four string parts and two wind parts) that I prepared in a notation program and then exported in MIDI format. You'll find more complete documentation, along with the download link for the software, at this Web page: homepage.mac.com/beryrinaldo/ddm/.

To use Dent du MIDI to bring MIDI files into GarageBand:

1. Start Dent du MIDI (**Figure 12.27**).

2. In the Finder, locate the MIDI file you want to import into GarageBand and arrange your windows so you can see the file's icon and the Dent du MIDI window at the same time (**Figure 12.28**).

3. Drag the MIDI file's icon into the Dent du MIDI window and release the mouse button (**Figure 12.29**).

continues on next page

BRINGING MIDI FILES INTO GARAGEBAND

After a short interval, "Completed" appears in the Dent du MIDI window.

4. Working in the Finder, click the window that contains the original MIDI file. A new folder appears, containing the AIFF files created by Dent du MIDI. Open this folder (**Figure 12.30**). It contains one AIFF file for each track in the MIDI file.

5. Make GarageBand the foreground application and place its window so that you can see both it and the folder that contains the converted files.

6. Drag the converted files into the timeline (**Figure 12.31**).

   After GarageBand finishes importing the files, each one is converted into a Software Instrument region in a newly created track.

7. Use the Track Info window to assign an instrument to each track (**Figure 12.32**).

✔ Tip

■ The program's name is a complicated bilingual pun—see the developer's Web page for the explanation.

Figure 12.30 The bottom window displays the files created by Dent du MIDI.

Figure 12.31 Dragging the files into GarageBand.

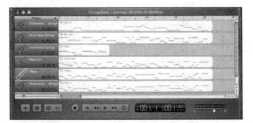

Figure 12.32 Each track has had an instrument assigned.

IMPROVING PERFORMANCE

As of this writing, GarageBand still shows all the normal signs of "version 1 syndrome": features that don't work quite as promised and lackluster performance. Apple, like most reputable software vendors, issues updates to its software from time to time with the goal of fixing bugs and making the program run more efficiently. So far, only one update to GarageBand has appeared (version 1.0.1), but hope springs eternal.

Run the Software Update application (found under the Apple menu) periodically to check for new versions of GarageBand. It's also a good idea to pay regular visits to the GarageBand support page at Apple's Web site (www.apple.com/support/garageband/), where you can check for software updates and search Apple's support database for answers to technical questions.

Another good resource for technical advice is the official GarageBand discussion board: discussions.info.apple.com/garageband/. GarageBand users gather here to share tips, report problems, and brainstorm to find solutions to the program's mysteries.

And finally, don't forget to let Apple know what you think about GarageBand. Use this page to submit complaints, suggestions, and words of praise: www.apple.com/feedback/garageband.html.

General Performance Tips

What's the one thing you can do that will have the biggest impact on GarageBand's performance?

Get a faster Mac.

No, seriously. The kind of data crunching GarageBand does is extremely processor intensive. The program requires at least a 600 MHz processor, but don't even think about using Software Instruments unless your Mac is powered by a G4 or G5 chip.

If a faster Mac doesn't happen to be in your budget at the moment, add as much RAM to your current machine as it will hold. The number of tracks GarageBand can handle at once is directly related to the amount of RAM installed.

You can also try to ensure that no other software is competing for your Mac's attention while running GarageBand. Here are some basic steps you can take (and what's great is that they don't cost any money):

◆ Make sure no other programs are running in the background while you're working in GarageBand.

◆ Turn off background system processes such as File Sharing.

◆ Disable timed application services that operate in the background, such as utilities that check for new e-mail messages periodically and scheduling programs that set off alarms to remind you of appointments.

◆ Turn off FileVault in System Preferences. If you can't do without the protection afforded by FileVault, you can safeguard your GarageBand songs by storing them somewhere other than in your Home folder (which includes your Documents and Music folders).

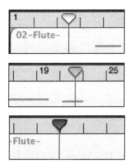

Figure A.1 Top: The color of the playhead at rest is plain white. Middle: The triangle shows a bit of color when playback is just starting to tax the processor. Bottom: The triangle is red, and GarageBand is in danger of coming to a crashing halt.

Monitor processor load with the playhead

The color of the triangle at the top of the playhead acts as an indicator of the amount of stress your hardware is experiencing while playing a song in GarageBand (**Figure A.1**). When the playhead is at rest, the triangle is blank, but during playback of your song, it changes color to alert you to conditions inside your machine. When you play a song with a few tracks, including some Software Instrument tracks, the triangle turns pale orange. The greater the load on the processor, the darker the color of the triangle. Finally, when GarageBand is about to collapse under the weight of the tasks you are asking it to perform, such as playing a song with many Software Instrument tracks and effects enabled, the triangle turns beet red. This is a warning that the program may be ready to stop dead in its tracks.

As your song plays, watch the playhead and note the places where the triangle darkens. Try thinning out the texture at those spots: trim (or delete) some regions from that neighborhood. Turning off effects helps lighten the load, too.

Reduce the graphics processing load

Apple makes beautiful interfaces for its software, but drawing all that eye candy on the screen is expensive in terms of processor cycles. In particular, it's the moving elements that exact the greatest penalty, so turning off or minimizing onscreen animation will gain a bit of breathing room for GarageBand. Here are some things to try:

◆ **Make the GarageBand window as small as possible.** The less of it there is to draw, the less effort it take to draw it,

continues on next page

GENERAL PERFORMANCE TIPS

right? To do this, drag the lower-right corner of the screen as far up and to the left as it will go (see "To resize the GarageBand window" in Chapter 1).

◆ **Zoom out until you can see the whole song.** Showing all the different colored regions marching across the screen from right to left takes quite a lot of processor horsepower. If the whole song is visible in the window, then nothing moves except the playhead. Use the zoom slider to accomplish this (see "Zooming in the Timeline" in Chapter 1).

◆ **Hide the track mixer column.** The little colored lights that make the track level meters a delight to watch also gobble up processor time. Click the triangle at the top of the Tracks column to tuck the Mixer column out of view (see "To hide the track mixer" in Chapter 3).

◆ **Hide the entire program while your song plays back.** Select Hide GarageBand from the GarageBand menu (or press Command-H).

Bounce tracks

If your song has enough tracks to cause your Mac to choke on playback, one solution is to *bounce* some of the tracks. Bouncing is a technique from analog recording days. It involves mixing down several tracks into a single track. This single track then takes the place of the tracks that were mixed to create it. See "Bouncing Tracks to Improve Performance" later in this chapter for detailed instructions.

Turn off unneeded effects

All instrument presets, whether Real Instruments or Software Instruments, come with a certain number of effects turned on by default. Each of these enabled effects

Figure A.2 These effects aren't doing you any good, but they're consuming valuable system resources.

saps some of your processor cycles. If your song won't play smoothly, open the Track Info window and examine the settings in the Details pane for each track (see "Applying Effects" in Chapter 10). Turn off effects that aren't absolutely necessary.

Be especially vigilant for effects that are turned on, but are turned all the way down (**Figure A.2**). These effects cost you processor time, too, even if their values are set to zero.

Allow fewer simultaneous notes in Software Instrument tracks

All Software Instrument tracks are not created equal when it comes to stressing your Mac during playback. A Software Instrument track used for a melody instrument, like a saxophone or bass, usually plays back only one note at a time. Keyboard and guitar tracks, on the other hand, frequently contain chords, which are stacks of notes sounding together.

Processing chords in a Software Instrument track makes GarageBand work harder than when it processes single-note tracks. You can set a limit on the number of notes an instrument can play at once using the Voices per Instrument pop-up menu in the Advanced pane of the GarageBand Preferences dialog. The default setting is Automatic, meaning that GarageBand decides how many voices to allot to each instrument based on the speed of your computer's CPU. To set a different limit, choose a setting from the Voices per Instrument menu. Notice that each of the choices allows twice as many notes for sampled instruments as for "other" (meaning synthesized) instruments. To read about the distinction between sampled and synthesized instruments, see "Real vs. Software Instrument Tracks" in Chapter 3.

To change the maximum number of voices per Software Instrument:

1. Choose GarageBand > Preferences (Command-,) to open the Preferences dialog.

2. Click the Advanced tab to switch to the Advanced preferences pane (**Figure A.3**).

3. From the Voices per Instrument pop-up menu, choose a different setting (**Figure A.4**).

   Settings allowing fewer notes improve GarageBand's playback performance, and settings allowing more voices per instrument are likely to degrade performance.

4. Close the Preferences dialog.

Figure A.3 The Advanced pane of the GarageBand Preferences dialog.

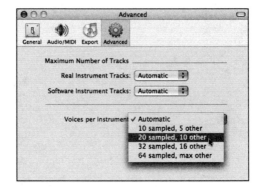

Figure A.4 The Voices per Instrument pop-up menu.

Figure A.5 This song has 10 Software Instrument tracks. Four of them are strings.

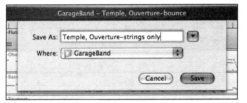

Figure A.6 Saving the file under a different name.

Bouncing Tracks to Improve Performance

Bouncing is a workaround that dates back to the days of analog tape recording. For example, if an engineer was working on a project that required 12 recorded tracks but had only 8-track equipment available, the solution was to combine, or *bounce*, some of those tracks into a single track. The bounced tracks could then be erased, leaving enough empty tracks for the rest of the song.

In GarageBand, bouncing comes in handy if your song uses more tracks than your Mac can gracefully handle. Start by building your song with a few tracks. Adjust the mix, save the file, and then export the song to iTunes (see "Exporting a Song to iTunes" in Chapter 12). Next, save the song under a new name, delete the tracks that you just exported, and find the exported song in the Finder and drag it into GarageBand. The material that required several tracks before now occupies only a single track.

This technique is especially useful if you use a lot of Software Instrument tracks, because they place much greater demands on the processing power of your system than do Real Instrument tracks. You can also bounce individual Software Instrument tracks to convert them to Real Instrument tracks, which allows you to increase the total number of tracks in your song.

To bounce tracks:

1. Refine the mix of your song and save the file (**Figure A.5**).

2. Use the Save As command to save a copy of your song under a new name.

   This is the copy you'll use to export tracks to iTunes (**Figure A.6**).

continues on next page

3. Delete all of the tracks that you don't want to be part of the bounced file. Unfortunately, GarageBand gives you no alternative but to delete them one by one, selecting each track in turn and pressing Command-Delete (**Figure A.7**).

4. Choose File > Export to iTunes and wait while GarageBand mixes and exports the tracks.

When the export process is complete, iTunes opens in the background.

5. Click the iTunes window to bring it to the foreground; then find the song you exported in your GarageBand export playlist (**Figure A.8**).

6. Select the song and Choose File > Show Song File (Command-R) to reveal the song file in the Finder (**Figure A.9**).

7. Open the original song file again. GarageBand will ask you if you want to save the file from which you deleted tracks in step 3. Click Don't Save.

Figure A.7 All of the wind, brass, and percussion tracks have been deleted, leaving only the string tracks.

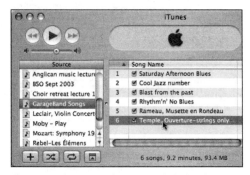

Figure A.8 The exported song is included in the GarageBand Songs playlist.

Figure A.9 The exported song file's Finder icon.

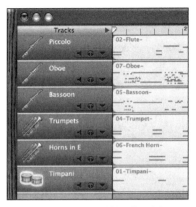

Figure A.10 The original file after deleting all four string tracks.

8. Delete the tracks you exported to iTunes in step 4 (**Figure A.10**).

9. Drag the exported song file into the GarageBand window (**Figure A.11**).

10. GarageBand creates a new track to hold the exported song (**Figure A.12**).

   The bounced tracks have been combined into a single Real Instrument track, reducing the total number of tracks in the song without losing any of the musical content in the bounced tracks.

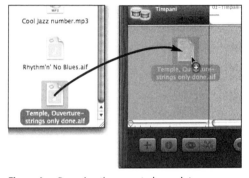

Figure A.11 Dragging the exported song into GarageBand.

Figure A.12 The exported song is placed in a new Real Instrument track.

The "Bounced" Bug

The GarageBand user forums at Apple's support Web site are full of reports of a peculiar phenomenon that can only be a bug: when the user exports a song to iTunes, the exported file is placed in a folder called Import, and the file itself is given the name Bounced.aif. Subsequent exports are named Bounced2.aif, Bounced3.aif, and so on.

There seems to be no sure-fire cure for this bug (other than an update to the software; please, Apple, while we're still young!), but some people have found that taking one or more of these actions clears up the problem:

♦ Sometimes, the export information in GarageBand's preferences file gets mangled. Open GarageBand's Preferences dialog and switch to the Export pane (see "To set export preferences" in Chapter 12). Clear the text in each field and enter new information; then close the dialog and restart GarageBand.

♦ The preferences file may be so corrupted that re-entering the export information won't help; you have to delete the entire preferences file and have GarageBand build a new one from scratch. Quit GarageBand; then open the folder /Users/[*your user name*]/Library/Preferences/ in the Finder and locate the file com.apple.garageband.plist. Drag this file to the Trash, empty the Trash, and then restart GarageBand and enter new export information in the Preferences dialog.

Note: If you follow this procedure, not only will all of your preferences be reset to default values, but you'll lose any information about favorite loops. Instrument and effects presets will not be lost, however.

♦ It's also possible that the ownership information for your iTunes Music folder has become garbled and needs to be fixed. To do this, run the Disk Utility program (in /Applications/Utilities), select your startup disk's icon in the left column, click the First Aid tab in the right column, and then click the Repair Disk Permissions button. When the process (which may take a while) finishes, close Disk Utility and restart your computer.

GARAGEBAND JAM PACK

Released simultaneously with the GarageBand program itself, the GarageBand Jam Pack is a collection of add-ons for GarageBand. Apple's marketing claims that the package includes "more than 2,000 additional Apple Loops in a variety of instruments, moods and genres, more than 100 new Software Instruments, over 100 audio effects presets and 15 new guitar amp settings." Plus, in early March 2004, Apple released GarageBand Jam Pack Update 1.0.1, which provided 17 new effects presets, indicated by asterisks (*) in the following list.

What, specifically, do you get for your $99?

A description or even a list of the 2,000 new Apple Loops is far beyond the scope of this book, but fortunately the intrepid duo of M. Danielson and Peter J. Hill at Macjams.com have posted a condensed listing of the loops, with descriptions, at www.macjams.com (see the article "In Depth: Apple GarageBand Jam Pack").

Generators (2)

Apple's boast of "more than 100 new Software Instruments" refers to generator presets. The number of new generators is much smaller—two, in fact.

♦ **Voice**

The Voice generator comes with one generator preset, Mixed Choir. Four Software Instrument presets use the Voice generator (see the following list). You'll find them all in the new Choir category.

♦ **Tuned Percussion**

The Tuned Percussion generator comes with three generator presets, which are based on two new sets of samples: Rotary Vibraphone and Vibraphone. The Tuned Percussion generator is used in seven new Software Instrument presets (see the following list) that have all been added to the Mallets category.

Generator Presets (101)

There is a good assortment of new generator presets. Here they are, grouped by generator:

Sampled presets (21)

Each of the new presets for sampled instruments comes with a folder of new samples. If you're curious, you can see them in /Library/Application Support/GarageBand/ Instrument Library/Sampler/Sampler Files/.

For example, the new Classical Piano preset uses sounds recorded from a fabulously expensive Bösendorfer piano, whose dark, mellow tone contrasts nicely with the brighter Yamaha piano used as the source for the samples in the Grand Piano preset.

- **Piano:** Classical Piano, Grand Piano+Bass, Grand Piano+Pad, Grand Piano+Strings

- **Strings:** Arco Strings, Pad Strings

- **Voice:** Mixed Choir

- **Tuned Percussion:** Rotary Vibraphone, Vibraphone+Bass, Vibraphone

- **Horns:** Funk Horn Section

- **Woodwind:** Baritone Sax, Classical Flute, Soprano Sax

- **Guitar:** 12 String Acoustic Chords, 12 String Acoustic Guitar, Muted Electric Guitar, Roundback Acoustic Guitar

- **Bass:** Ballad Electric Bass, Picked Electric Bass, Upright Ballad Bass

- **Drum Kits:** Electro Kit, RnB Kit, Tribal Kit

Synthesized presets (80)

No new software components were added with the new synthesizes presets. These are merely new collections of settings for each synthesizer generator.

- **Analog Basic:** Blue Sky Synth, Bright Square Bass, Classic Brass, Fat Sequence, Hard Octave, Rezzy Brass, Ringtone, RnB Bass, Slow Brass, Soft Pulse Lead, Square Bass, Super Octave

- **Analog Mono:** Dirty Sweller, Fat Pulsbass, Mini Bass 3, Mini Crusher, Mini Lead 3, Mini Lead 4, New Luck, Sonic Lead, Wow Bass

- **Analog Pad:** Atmo Pad 3, Bright Pad, Dark Pad ModW, Digi Synth, HiPass ModW, HPF Sweep , Perc Digisyn, Phasing HiPaStabs, Phasing MixStabs, Softsyn

- **Analog Swirl:** Avantgarde, Blue Lead, Bright Swell, No Resonance Pad, Popular Synth, PWM Lead, PWM Percussive Synth, Synth Sheep, Tacky

- **Analog Sync:** Groovy Sync, Nirvana, Sync Lead C, Sync Lead D, Sync Pad C, Sync Pad D, Syncy

- **Digital Basic:** Bitcrush Keys, Digital Synth B, FM Bells C, FM Percussion C, FM Percussion D, FM Warmsynth, Glassy Pad 2, Metallic Atmo C, Metallic Atmo D, Tremolo Bells

- **Digital Mono:** Hard Corer, Impact Bass, Metal Slapper, Perc X, Power Fuzz, Rope Man, Steam Hammer

- **Digital Stepper:** Chorus Organ B, Crosswaves C ModW, Dark Crosswaves, Filter RNDM, Mellow Blue, Mystical, PWM Stringpad, Saw Pad, Voodoo Groove A, Zero Lima

- **Tonewheel Organ:** Cathedral (less), Dust, Simple Organ

Effects Presets (52)

The new effects presets are something of a mixed bag. Some effects get lots of new presets, and others get very few (or none, in the case of the Bass Reduction effect). The Jam Pack Update 1.0.1 fleshed out the list quite a bit, beefing up the original number of presets by 50 percent.

- **Treble Reduction:** Ultra*

- **Equalizer:** Add Bass Clarity, Add Bass Punch*, Air Vocals, Enhance Bass Drum*, Harder Guitars, Improve Thin Sounds*, Reduce Bass Boom, Remove Guitar Dullness*, Soft Background Vocals*

- **Overdrive:** Drive 4*

- **Bitcrusher:** AM Radio, Sample Rate Crusher

- **Automatic Filter:** Club Next Door, Deep and Slow Filter, Eight Notes Dark Pulse, Fast Pulse, Fast Saw Filter, Resonance Ticks, Triple Offset Filter

- **Chorus:** Atmospheric*, Deep Modulation, Glimmer, Jazz Chorus*

- **Flanger:** Dolphin Flange*, Fascination*, Intergalactic Police*, Laser Fire*, Modulating, Slow Sweep, Stadium Flange, Super Flange*

- **Phaser:** Funk Phase, Harmonic Filter*, Living, Phrasator, Rock Phaser*, Vocoder Phase, Wild Phase

- **Tremolo:** Deep Slow Pan, Fast Mono Tremolo, Light Pan, Rotor Robot, Rotor Vox, Soft Tremolo

- **Auto Wah:** Funky Filter, Hi Reaction, Strong Gate

- **Amp Simulation:** American Lead, British Clean, British Overdrive

Instrument Presets (178)

The Jam Pack also includes 178 new instrument presets, but no new master track presets. You'll find the "15 new guitar amp settings" advertised by Apple listed under "Guitars" among the Real Instrument presets. Here are all of the new instrument presets, listed by type and by category.

Software Instrument presets (126)

- **Bass:** Ballad Electric Bass, Chain Saw Bass, Chirp Synth Bass, Deep & Hard Bass, Driving Synth Bass, Eighties Pop Synth Bass, Electric Upright Jazz, Filter Wah Synth Bass, Fretless Solo Bass, Funky Filter Bass, Hammer Synth Bass, Nasty Synth Bass, Picked Electric Bass, Pulse Synth Bass, Underground Synth Bass, Upright Ballad Bass

- **Choir:** Alien Glow, Basking Glow, Mixed Choir, Olympus Voices

- **Drum Kits:** Android Kit, Electro Kit, Hip Hop Kit, Jazz Kit, Laser Kit, RnB Kit, Telephone Kit, Tribal Kit, Twang Kit

- **Guitars:** 12 String Acoustic, 12 String Chords, Auditorium Acoustic, Ballad Acoustic, Chorus Roundback, Delicate Echoes, Edgy Muted, Funky Wah, Muted Electric, Roundback Acoustic, Textural Electric

- **Horns:** Funk Horn Section, Live Funk Horns, Radio Horns, Synth Horn Section, Wah Horns

- **Mallets:** Caribbean Vibraphone, Rotary Vibraphone, Solo Vibraphone, Space Vibraphone, Tremolophone, Vibraphone and Bass, Vibraphone

- **Organs:** Circus Organ, Gospel Organ, Heavy Metal Organ, Lounge Organ, Modulating Synth Organ, Old Radio Organ, Percussive Organ, Rock Organ, Soul Organ, Space Organ, Sparkling Organ, Toy Organ, Vocoder Synth Organ

- **Pianos and Keyboards:** Ambient Synth Piano, Chorused Electric Piano, Classical Piano, Dark Clav, Echo Piano, Fuzz Clav, Live Classical Piano, Live Grand Piano, Moody Grand Piano, Phased Clav, Piano and Bass, Piano and Strings, Seventies Electric Piano, Tremolo Whirly

- **Strings:** Bright Arco Strings, Orchestral Arco Strings, Satellite Strings, Solace

- **Synth Basics:** Bubble Gum Brass, Chime Synth, Dramatic Moment, Dreamy Bells, Eighties Sci-Fi, Electron Collisions, Escape Velocity, Looking Glass, Neutrino Pulse, Sequence Element 3, Sequence Element 4, Sequence Element 5, Sequence Element 6, Sequence Element 7, Sequence Element 8, Techno Chirper, UFO Cycler

- **Synth Leads:** All Swell, Digital Brass, Fifth Moon, Funk City, Funky Octavia, Lightning Rod, Lost in Trance, Pressured Air, Stratospheric

- **Synth Pads:** Analog Swell, Android Engine, Atmosphere Artifacts, Caffeine Trance, Cinematic Sillouhette, Cybernetic Bulkhead, Electric Slumber, Elven Breath, Heavenly Glass, Icy Whirlpool, Liquid Oxygen, Romulan Raindrops, Solar Flare, Tranquil Horizon, Underwater Turnstyle

- **Woodwinds:** Arctic Wind, Baritone Sax, Classical Flute, Soprano Sax

continues on next page

Real Instrument presets (52)

- ◆ **Band Instruments:** Baritone Sax, Live Horn Section, Old Vinyl Brass, Tenor Sax, Trumpet Solo, Warm Strings

- ◆ **Bass:** Colorful Bass, Edgy Bass, Filter Bass, Grind Bass, Hi Hop Bass, Modulating Bass, Sparkle Bass, Tight Acoustic Bass, Tight Bass, Wave Bass

- ◆ **Drums:** Element Isolator, Fade Out Drums, Isolate Sub Bass Drum, Low Res Drums, Quarter Pulse Drums, Vocoder Drums

- ◆ **Effects:** Atari Sings, Celestial Spring, Intense Whispering, Lunar Bounce, Orion Vocals, Wandering Around, Zapper

- ◆ **Guitars:** Barroom Lead, Bright Country, Eighties Pop, Funky Rhythm, Grunge, Heavy Blues, Indie Rock, Liverpool Clean, Metal, Scorching Solo, Seventies Rhythm, Summer Sounds, Surf, Texas Blues, Ultra Clean

- ◆ **Vocals:** Female Dance Vocals, Female RnB Vocals, Gospel Choir, Male Dance Vocals, Male RnB Vocals, Male Speech, Megaphone, Radio Effect

INDEX

INDEX